# THE COMPLETE GUIDE TO CROSS-COUNTRY SKI PREPARATION

## NAT BROWN

THE
MOUNTAINEERS

Published by
The Mountaineers
1001 SW Klickitat Way, Suite 201
Seattle, WA 98134

© 1999 by Nat Brown    796.932
                       BRO

First edition, 1999

Published simultaneously in Great Britain by Cordee, 3a DeMontfort Street, Leicester, England, LE1 7HD

Manufactured in the United States of America

Edited by Jane C. Crosen
Cover design and book design by Ani Rucki
Book layout by Anne Treadwell

*Library of Congress Cataloging-in-Publication Data*
Brown, Nat, 1948–
    The complete guide to cross-country ski preparation / Nat Brown. — 1st ed.
        p.        cm.
    Includes index.
    ISBN 0-89886-600-6 (pbk.)
    1. Ski waxing. 2. Cross-country skiing. I. Title.
GV855.5.W39 B76 1999
796.93'2—dc21                              99-6249
                                           CIP

# CONTENTS

*To my father, Edmond L. Brown,*

*and*

*Jim Galanes*

# PREFACE

A few words about how this book came to be.

I was fortunate enough to work as waxing coach for the U.S. Biathlon Team in the 1987 World Championship season, and again during the 1988 Olympic season, waxing and preparing skis. The 1987 season was something of a shock: Josh Thompson took a silver medal at the World Championships in Lake Placid, becoming the first American ever to win a medal in the Biathlon, and the only American other than Bill Koch (silver, 1976 Olympics) ever to medal in a Nordic sport.

Shortly after Lake Placid, Josh and I found ourselves in Europe, representing the United States in the remaining 1987 World Cup and Polar Cup races. I had done a lot of waxing and ski preparation at the divisional level, but suddenly I found myself in the deep end of the pool. With patience on Josh's part, and a certain amount of beginner's luck, I did some fast learning about nonstop ski preparation at the highest level of competition, and Josh had some extremely fast skis. At the World Cup finale in Lillehammer, he ran the first leg of the relay for the Norwegian "B" Team and came in to the tag in second place, just behind the DDR (East Germany), ahead of Norway's "A" Team!

The next year, I was hired as part of the Olympic Preparation program, to wax and prepare skis for the entire Biathlon Team. With a whole team to take care of, I knew it was time to do some hard thinking and start coming up with an organized, systematic method of testing waxes and skis and preparing bases. I began to work directly with some of the wax and ski companies and received help from several foreign wax coaches, notably Magne Myrmo, who was then waxing skis for Norway. At the end of the season I wrote the original version of this book.

At that time there was no systematic, in-depth book on ski preparation available to the skiing public, and one was needed that would attempt to deal with the many questions I was getting almost every day. I didn't know much more than the people who were asking me questions, but I did have the contacts to get some answers and the time to do a lot of testing and trying. So I wrote and self-published the first version of this book, about half the length of the current one, in an effort to pass on what I was learning.

Since then I have continued to be fortunate in both the opportunities I've had to learn, and the people with whom I've been able to work. In 1989 Steve Gaskill hired me to take over waxing and ski preparation for the U.S. Cross-Country Team, with Jim Galanes as my supervisor. That was when I really began to learn—partly from Jim's huge store of knowledge and experience, and partly because of his refusal to accept as final any answers that we couldn't prove. We tested over 2,000 wax combinations, talked with representatives from all the wax companies, prepped and tested endless pairs of skis, and continually refined our testing methods. One day at Les Saisies, during the 1992 Olympics, we made ninety-eight trips up and down the test hill before it got too dark to go on testing—almost 10 kilometers of skiing just on the test hill.

One result of all this was my growing awareness of the inadequacy of the first book: I was learning so much, and so many new materials and techniques were emerging. I began to rewrite and expand the book at the end of every season, adding new material and throwing out what had become out-of-date or been proved wrong.

I parted company with the U.S. Cross-Country Team in 1993 and began to freelance, working with Belgium and with the Slovene Ski Team. In 1997 I began to work with Lars Svensson, who does stone-grinding for most of the top skiers in the world. Lars and I plan to work together at least through 2002 and the Salt Lake City Olympics—there's still more to learn!

In the spring of 1998 The Mountaineers agreed to publish the book at its current stage of evolution. Editor-in-Chief Margaret Foster paired me with editor Mark Long, and together he and I reorganized the material into its present state. Getting published by The Mountaineers is a relief: at last I can stop rewriting and pass on a great deal of information that fortunately has come my way.

I still don't claim to know all the answers. Indeed, the more I learn, the more I am humbled by how much there is yet to learn . . . how much more people like Jim Galanes and Lars Svensson already know . . . and how much time and energy people like them are putting into the research that brings our knowledge of skiing forward. But I do believe that this book can serve as a coherent source of techniques and knowledge useful for skiers at virtually all skill levels.

I hope skiers will find *The Complete Guide to Cross-Country Ski Preparation* as interesting to read as it was to write.

—*Nat Brown*

# ACKNOWLEDGMENTS

I have dedicated both editions of this book to my father, Edmond L. Brown, who gave me a love of tools and a respect for their proper use, and served as well as an inspiring example of patient and careful craftsmanship in its finest sense. But I must credit as well another person who has taught me what seems like everything I know about skiing: Jim Galanes, my supervisor in ski preparation for the U.S. Cross-Country Team. Jim made me learn in the years when I was fortunate enough to work with him, and through his untiring devotion to finding the best possible solution he has remained an inspiration ever since. My life would be much poorer without both of these wonderful teachers.

In addition, I'd like to thank Peter Hale, who has been a long-suffering friend, generous supporter, and indefatigable colleague for twenty years, and Mark Long, my editor, without whose patient and detailed work none of this would make sense.

# INTRODUCTION

*... The end of all our exploring*
*Will be to arrive where we started*
*And know the place for the first time.*
                    T. S. Eliot, "Little Gidding"

In March 1990 I was in Ornsköldsvik, Sweden, for the final World Cup races that had been moved there from a snowless Falun.

At that point in the World Cup, the world's dominant skier, Sweden's Gunde Svan, was leading over Norway's Vegard Ulvang by a narrow margin, but everyone assumed that Gunde had the overall World Cup title all sewn up.

The Swedes missed the wax, however, and their top finisher, Christer Majbäck, was twentieth, over 3 minutes behind the winner, Norway's Terje Langli. Gunde finished fiftieth, probably the worst finish in his life, and lost the World Cup to Vegard.

What happened?

My records show that the humidity was medium, the air temperature was +4°C, and the snow was -2°C, fresh, and showing signs of glazing in the track. It was a classic, or diagonal race (as opposed to a skating race), so we applied several layers of violet kick wax to our skis and had excellent reports of how our skis were working: lots of kick, good glide—nice skiing, in fact.

The Swedes had put sticky Chola klister binder on their skis, and applied the hard wax over it. The result was a mess that would neither kick nor glide. "The Swedish Ski Games 30-kilometer was a fiasco," as the March 12 edition of *Sporten* put it.

What *really* happened? My guess is that too many wax coaches were trying to be the one to come up with the dynamite combination, and in the process, things got too complicated. They lost sight of the first rule of waxing:

## KEEP IT SIMPLE!

This rule is so important that I bear the acronym "KISS" ("Keep It Simple, Skier!") in mind all the time when waxing. Keep simplicity

9

in mind, and you will never go far astray in preparing and waxing skis. I promise.

This book is designed to bring the reader to simplicity in waxing and ski preparation through an understanding of the principles and techniques involved in choosing the right ski, and getting it ready for optimal performance. Readers are invited to view the book as a systematic "course" in ski preparation, starting at the most basic level, and progressing through all the techniques needed to produce really fast skis. The book is divided into three parts.

**Part 1** covers the basics: going to the store to buy a pair of skis, and how to pick the right ones for *you*. We'll discuss what they're made of—especially the bases—and then we'll have a look at snow and how it affects skis and wax. And finally, we'll find out why wax works.

**Part 2** begins by asking the question "What makes a ski slow?" Then we'll examine one by one all the factors that can affect a ski's ability to glide, and go over ways to minimize or eliminate them. In other words, we'll learn the practical techniques of ski preparation: use of the scraper, flattening the base, applying structure, waxing, and final preparation.

**Part 3** will branch into more advanced areas such as waxing safety, new developments in waxing, testing skis and wax, and ski repair.

The final section of the book will be appendixes with suggested tool lists, sources for waxes and equipment, suggested test forms, and a glossary of terms.

Keep It Simple, Skier!

## Measurements Used in This Book

The ski world is metric: we race in kilometers, and most waxing products are rated in Celsius degrees only. Conversion information for the most common measurements is provided here.

To convert Celsius to Fahrenheit, multiply by ⅘ and then add 32; to convert Fahrenheit to Celsius, subtract 32 and multiply by ⅚.

|  |  |  |
|---|---|---|
| 0°C | 32°F | freezing point of water |
| 10°C | 50°F | |
| 20°C | 68°F | |
| 30°C | 86.8°F | |
| 40°C | 104°F | |
| 50°C | 122°F | |
| 60°C | 140°F | |
| 70°C | 158°F | |
| 80°C | 176°F | |
| 90°C | 194°F | |
| 100°C | 212°F | boiling point of water |

| | |
|---|---|
| 25 millimeters (2.5 centimeters) | 1 inch |
| 1 meter | 1.1 yard |
| 1 kilometer | 0.6 mile |

| | |
|---|---|
| 1 gram | 0.035 ounce |
| 1 kilogram | 2.2 pounds |

# Part 1

# BASICS

The first part of this book might be called the "mechanical" part, in which we will take a look at the basics that underlie getting the most out of our skis. We will start at the beginning, picking out the right skis for you and the conditions in which you'll be skiing, and this will involve some discussion of the mechanics of how a ski works. Then we will move on to considering the material the ski bases are made of and how it affects our choice of skis. Finally, we will look at the environment of skiing—snow— and gain an understanding of how wax works.

# CHOOSING THE RIGHT SKIS

Getting the most out of skiing begins with choosing the right skis. The proper pair of skis will be faster and easier to control than a poorly chosen pair. More importantly, the right skis will add an extra dimension of pleasure to your skiing.

For top racers, who must win those few seconds between a gold medal and placing down in the list, matching the ski to the skier and to the specific conditions is vital. For the citizen racer, whose ability to test skis and whose range of available choices may be more limited, the process is simpler. But even if you are buying a pair of no-wax skis for an occasional outing, having the right skis can make the difference between a positive experience you will want to repeat, and one that can leave you with a negative impression of this wonderful sport.

So, let's begin at the very beginning: choosing the right skis.

## Self-Evaluation

The first thing you need to do when buying new skis is to evaluate yourself and your own capabilities. Remember: be honest with yourself in order to enjoy skiing.

**Economy.** Decide whether you want to buy the most expensive skis or prefer a more economical alternative. There are good skis on the market that are not too expensive.

**Use.** What do you need from a ski? Decide whether you want a classic (diagonal) or a skating ski (see the specific guidelines for choosing skis later in this chapter), and whether you need the skis for powder or for wet snow. Try to define what has worked well for you in the past. Good skis that are to be replaced can be taken along to the shop in order to try to find a pair with the same flex characteristics.

**Age.** Younger skiers who are just starting should have a softer ski.

**Weight/height.** Your weight is important in your choice of skis. If we look at weight alone, a person who weighs 60 kilograms should have a "softer," or more flexible, ski than one who weighs 70 kilograms. As far as height goes, the rule of thumb is that a classic ski should equal your height plus 30 centimeters. Skating skis should be 10 to 15 centimeters shorter than classic skis.

**Technique/condition.** These are very important when deciding how stiff a ski you should use. A skier with good technique who is in top physical condition can use a stiffer ski, but remember that you have to be able to put the ski down against the snow when you are tired. If you have a late kick, for example, you should choose a softer ski.

You should also be aware that ski companies have developed wet-snow and powder-snow skis, with special bases for the various conditions. Be sure you are buying the ski that meets your needs.

## General Guidelines for Choosing Skis

Following are some guidelines for buying a new pair of skis. Some of the techniques described will require some practice and experience, but you will quickly gain confidence by following the steps below. Observe the characteristics of the skis you already have that work well for you, and then "just do it"—go into a shop and compare a lot of pairs and several brands of skis. You can also seek assistance from a knowledgeable salesperson, but the point here is to develop *your* ability to choose a good ski. Remember: the goal is to increase your enjoyment of skiing. It's a fantastic experience to ski on skis that really fit.

First, place the skis together, base to base. Squeeze them firmly. If they splay at the tip (spread apart), you will not get even pressure distribution along the length of the skis. A little splay may be allowed in soft-snow skis, but beware the ski with much splay; it will be unstable and slow.

Holding the skis together, sight down along their length as you squeeze: they should come together evenly. If one ski flattens

*Figure 1. Sighting down a pair of skis to see if they close evenly.*

more easily than the other, it is not a properly matched pair (figure 1).

Still holding the skis together, squeeze a little and place the flat of your hand between the tips to feel softness or hardness. Check tip and tail flex by (gently) bending the ski. Too stiff a tip can be slow; ideally, good all-purpose skis should be softer in the tip than in the tail, and the curve of both should be even as you apply pressure.

When you go shopping for skis, take along a flat edge, such as a steel scraper or truing bar, to check for a uniformly flat bottom surface. Place the tool across the ski on the shovel area and the tail area; in fact, check the entire length, as shown in figure 2. A little concavity or convexity may be tolerated at the tip and tail, and can often be scraped out. Large aberrations are to be avoided; if nothing else, they will make the ski hard to work on because it will be hard to reach into the "hollow" with an iron or a scraper. Note that some degree of concavity is expected on either side of a pressed (round) groove, and can sometimes be scraped out. A concavity just at the tail does not matter much; this is a low-pressure area.

Look for obvious flaws—gouges, dents, etc.—and make sure the groove is straight. Even the best-controlled manufacturing passes the occasional flawed ski. On the other hand, if the ski is a good one, with good flex patterns, don't worry about the odd dent or scratch; these will have little effect on the ski's speed. It is far more important to have a ski that works for you! In the late 1980s, World Championship silver medalist Josh Thompson had one pair of Landsem skis that were rockets in most conditions. Although they eventually picked up a number of gouges and dents, they remained an extraordinarily good pair until the day Josh changed to another ski brand and they were retired. They now reside in my garage, and when we took them out for a spin for the first time in nine years, they were still going. The moral: A fast ski is a fast ski is a fast ski.

Be sure to check manufacturers' recommendations for specific weight range and snow type. Many shops now have testing devices provided by the various manufacturers that will help you to make this choice. (If you're on your own in terms of flex testing, see the testing recommendations discussed below under "Choosing Classic Skis").

Some retailers specialize in matching skis to the owner's needs and weight. However, be aware that as the season progresses, stocks diminish and choice becomes more limited. It is a good idea to choose and order your skis early.

*Figure 2. Using a steel scraper to check a base for flatness—sight along the base and look for light under the scraper.*

The most important thing to remember when choosing a ski is that the ski must fit you and your needs, so that you will continue to ski and enjoy skiing, regardless of your level.

Again, all of these methods require practice, along with reference to skis that you know work well for you in various conditions. Just do it! Wade in, and learn.

## Choosing Classic Skis

The **wax pocket** of a classic ski—the area in the middle of a classic ski where you apply kick wax—is the most important part of the ski. A wax pocket that suits your skiing and the conditions is the most critical consideration in finding a ski that will give you the best and most enjoyable skiing experience.

A classic ski is not built simply as a long curve; it will usually have a "second camber," a pocket in the center of the ski which is much harder to flatten out. (**Camber** is a word used to describe the stiffness, or flex, of a ski. The curve of a ski as it lies on a flat surface is related to its stiffness and feel, and is also referred to as camber.) This "second camber" is the wax pocket, and its function is to keep the kick wax, which will act as a drag when in contact with the snow, off the track except during the actual kick. There are two basic camber profiles, those of klister skis and of powder skis.

**Klister skis** will tend to have a shorter wax pocket, which will be stiffer than the pocket on a powder ski. Because klister has excellent traction characteristics (only a short area of the base needs to be covered with klister) but tends both to drag and pick up dirt, pine needles, etc., the ski is designed to keep the klister off the snow.

**Powder skis** will tend to have a longer, softer pocket; this is because the wax is harder and you need more of it to grip. At the same time, hard waxes glide better than klisters when in contact with the snow, so you can afford a softer ski.

Establishing a wax pocket is the most important part of finding the right ski for your needs, both in terms of glide and in terms of uphill skiing, which is perhaps even more important.

### Finding the Wax Pocket

The following are three valuable tests you can perform yourself to establish a ski's camber profile, or wax pocket.

**The squeeze test.** The squeeze test is a good one to start with, and can be done in the ski shop.

Squeeze the skis together, applying force with your hands approximately where the ball of the foot would be. Look where the ski closes when you squeeze hard. If the closure is about at the heel, well and good (don't wax behind this point). If the closure is much farther back, the chances are you may have an unforgiving ski that may be hard to make climb. Waxing back of the heel may be indicated for better kick, and it will not affect glide.

**The paper test.** You can proceed to the paper test after eliminating a number of pairs by squeezing them. A well-equipped shop may have some sort of ski testing apparatus designed specifically for flex testing, which will do the same thing as the paper test, but many shops do not, so facility with this test (figure 3) is a valuable skill to develop.

1. Lay the ski on a flat surface with a piece of paper placed under the balance point.
2. Stand on both skis (even weight distribution) with the ball of the foot located about 7 centimeters behind the balance point. It should be easy to move the paper.

*Figure 3. The paper test will indicate if the skis are the right flex, as well as help you to find the kick wax zones on classic skis. Be sure to use a smooth, flat surface!*

3. Stand on both skis (as above). It should be possible to move the paper 20–25 centimeters forward of the binding, and 5–10 centimeters back of the heel.
4. Put all your weight onto one ski, up on the ball of the foot. In the case of a powder ski, it should now be difficult to move the paper. With klister skis, on the other hand, you should still be able to move the paper somewhat; how much depends upon your technique and physical condition.

**The wax test.** The wax test is for fine-tuning your skis. Do this test out on the track after buying the skis and mounting the bindings.

Apply kick wax over a length longer than the anticipated wax pocket. Ski far enough to wear off some wax, then look at the base. The area where the wax has worn off, from front to back, defines the real wax pocket.

A variation on this test is to wax too long, then stop every kilometer or so and remove a centimeter of wax with a spatula; when kick is suddenly reduced and/or glide suddenly improves, you are in the wax pocket.

Once you have defined the wax pocket, you can mark the zone on the sidewalls of your skis, as described under "Proper Flex."

## Choosing Skating Skis

Skating skis are built on the same principle as classic skis, with stiff skis for wet snow, and softer skis for powder. It is important to note that skating skis have a wider area of application than classic skis, because kick wax is eliminated. For example, wet-snow skis are often very effective in colder conditions on hard tracks.

Skating skis are constructed with a stiffer middle section than classic skis. This is done to distribute body weight evenly over a shorter ski. It is therefore important to find a ski with an even transition from the stiffer middle part to the softer tip and tail areas. If the transition is too abrupt, it can act as a brake.

Skating skis can be roughly divided into soft, medium, and stiff. Any serious ski shop should have a stiffness chart or table with complete information on stiffness for various weight groups and conditions. Be sure to use this information when you choose skating skis.

A good skating ski will have a deep groove, or multiple grooves— important for the ski's stability—and sharp edges for good purchase in the skating phase. The ski should work *with* you, not against you.

## Skis for Younger Skiers

It is important that those responsible for choosing skis for children be aware of their responsibility. It is extremely important that younger skiers enjoy skiing and being out in the woods and fields. Properly fitted equipment is fundamental for enjoyment!

It is better for younger skiers to grow out of skis than into them. Longer skis are constructed with heavier skiers in mind. When a child who has to use skis too long for him spins his wheels regardless of what wax has been put on, there is little chance that he will develop an interest in skiing—and the path to other sports is very short.

## Skis for the Top Racer

For the top racer, ski choice is just as important as the wax for good results. At spring and fall on-snow camps, teams and company reps prioritize testing of ski construction, trying to match them to each skier's technique.

For example, one skier may have a classic technique that requires kick wax under the heel to keep him from slipping; this means that the back end of the camber curve has to be softer. Another racer may need a completely different kind of ski. Some skiers will prefer a longer camber, some a shorter camber (see "Choosing Classic Skis," above).

Development of better skis continues all the time, at high speed. For top racers, it can be important to try to keep on top of the newest developments. But for citizen racers and recreational skiers, it is better to forget all this complicated stuff: as skis develop through testing, the manufacturers quickly pass improvements on to the buying public.

The important thing is that the ski has to work for *you*. Concentrate on classic skis that function as well as possible when you are skiing *uphill and in hilly terrain, and not just when gliding downhill!* In an hour of skiing you actually don't ski downhill for more than 5–8 minutes. You can earn seconds on skis that go well down-hill, but on the other hand, you can lose minutes in the uphills.

At the top level, arriving at skis that fit the individual involves a great deal of testing. Some skiers have tested as many as 150 pairs of skis, counting both styles. At the World Championships in Val di Fiemme in 1991, Swedish ski giant Gunde Svan and his service man Ferry Grill tested 400 pairs! Others are pleased after ten to fifteen pairs. Testing is a lot of work, but good racers realize how important it is to compete on the best equipment.

Now that I've said all this, remember that most skiers will still be using many of their old "war horses" in any given season. In 1997 we waxed up Josh Thompson's 1987 silver medal skis for him to use at a clinic—and they were still the fastest skis there!

I always try to lower the number of skis per athlete. It is difficult if you have four or five pairs to worry about up until the start. The basic principle is: One good pair for cold weather, one for "zero conditions," and one for klister conditions. (**Klister** is a sticky wax that comes in "toothpaste" tubes. It is designed for use in snow that has melted and refrozen, or when much water is present. We'll look at klisters and their applications in Chapter 12.)

## Proper Flex

For those interested in the technical considerations behind the simpler recommendations presented above, the following presents a more in-depth look at determining the appropriate flex pattern. Skiers not interested in the more intricate, technical side of ski selection should feel free to skip this section.

Here we will discuss choosing the proper pair of skis based on the camber curve produced by the Compuflex test machine. I am indebted to Johan Landsem for much of the following information.

The Compuflex machine consists of a flat steel surface against which the ski is pressed until flat, or "closed." The amount of pressure it takes to flatten the ski is then recorded, and the pressure is gradually released, allowing the ski to rise from the flat surface. As the pressure is let off, instruments measure how much of the ski has risen from the flat surface. The resulting graph might show, for example, that the ski closed at 75 kilograms, that at 70 kilograms the ski had lifted off at points 10 centimeters ahead of and behind the pressure point (which is usually the balance point), that at 65 kilograms the ski lifted off at 15 centimeters ahead and 12 centimeters behind the pressure point, and so on. What is measured, then, is the pressure distribution of the ski.

In choosing a ski, two points in the curve are especially important: (1) the top point of the curve, and (2) the camber length at half the skier's weight. The top point of the curve represents the pressure needed to flatten the ski onto the snow, which relates to the ski's gripping capabilities. In the case of classic skis, good kick is needed on both flats and uphills. Generally speaking, in dry snow, a skier with a weight of 70 kilograms (154 pounds) should have a top point close to 56 kilograms (123 pounds), or 80 percent of body weight, and a camber length of 40 centimeters at half of body weight (35 kilograms, or 77 pounds). This skier could also pick skis with a camber length of 60 centimeters at half of body weight, but in this case the top point should be lowered to 60 percent of body weight, or about 42 kilograms (92 pounds).

As the thermometer nears 0°C, and a wax softer than extra-blue is called for, the skier can improve glide by choosing a ski with the highest possible top point and substantially shorter camber length at half of body weight.

When conditions dictate use of a soft wax for kick, the camber must be such that the wax touches the snow as little as possible while gliding (half of the weight on each ski).

It is not enough for the ski to have a camber length of 40–50 centimeters at half of body weight. It must also have the proper height of camber at the same loading. The height of the camber relates to how quickly the entire glide surface comes in contact with the snow during the diagonal stride.

### Recommended Camber Height

Klister skis:   at full body weight, 0.8–1 mm
                at half body weight, 1.4–1.8 mm
Powder skis:    at full body weight, 0 mm
                at half body weight, 0.6–1 mm

At 0°C and in conditions where wax softer than extra-blue is called for, a ski should be chosen somewhere between the values above.

Important in choosing a ski are the following:
- camber length at 50 percent of the skier's weight
- camber height at above 50 percent of the skier's weight
- camber length to above 50 percent of the skier's weight

Good klister skis (red klister conditions) should have a camber height between 0.8 and 1 millimeter, and a camber length of 20–30 centimeters at the skier's full weight. For effective kick, the camber length at 50 percent of body weight should not exceed 45–50 centimeters, in order to avoid the klister coming in contact with the snow in the glide phase, when the ski is loaded at full weight. *Skiers who wish to race at the highest levels must learn to ski on stiff skis when conditions call for them.*

Skating skis generally call for the same norms as classic skis. However, because kick is not necessary, you should pick slightly stiffer skis than for classic. In powder snow, pressure against the track should be even along the entire base, but in wet snow we get the best glide with less glide surface; that is, if the middle part is not pressed against the snow.

Proper identification of the wax pocket is very important to getting the best out of your skis. The three methods for identifying the pocket, as outlined above, should be part of a careful, ongoing process until you are genuinely sure you know your kick zone (or zones; skiers with a pair of skis they use for both klister and hard wax will want to identify two separate zones). Experiment, adjust, and do it early in the season, not when racing starts!

Be sure to mark your wax zones clearly, best done by marking the sidewalls with a marker pen, or even some paint.

Now let's have a look at ski construction, or at least the part that relates most directly to ski waxing: the base.

# 2
## Chapter

# SKI BASES

Cross-country skis come with a bewildering range of base types. In this chapter, we'll have a look at different types of base materials with the intent of simplifying the process of choosing the ski type that works best for you. Our focus will not be the technical aspects of ski construction but rather how the base affects waxing by absorbing or diffusing heat, warping under heat, etc.

Keep in mind that the ski producer wants you to be pleased with your skis, and has taken great pains to match you to the ski and the ski to the snow. Read the manufacturer's recommendations, and *keep it simple.*

## Wood and the "Fiberglass Revolution"

The high-tech equipment used today bears very little resemblance to the skis we used before 1974. In the 1974 World Championships held in Falun, Sweden, Swedish skier Thomas Magnusson became the first skier to race on fiberglass skis. He won the 30-kilometer race by 53 seconds, and wood was dead. Within a season, those beautiful and patiently constructed pieces of wood were completely gone from the international racing scene.

But it is just as well. While wood skis were cheaper (I outfitted my first team on closeouts for $1.79 per pair!), they were fragile, and the wood on the bases soaked up water; plus wood fiber "hair" could make for very slow skis, especially in wet snow. The new skis, with polyethylene, or P-Tex bases, were much faster.

P-Tex had been used for alpine skis for years before Nordic ski manufacturers made the switch from wood. It was a crucial improvement. The introduction of "all-fiberglass skis" (which actually contain other materials, including wood, Kevlar, foams, and aluminum honeycomb) paved the way to much more break-resistant skis, and made it possible to experiment with all kinds of constructions that would make skis stiffer, especially torsionally, able to hold their shape and camber indefinitely.

Today, P-Tex bases are used on almost all racing skis, and most racing skis now have "sintered" bases, which allows for better wax penetration. Different types of P-Tex have been developed which function better in different conditions. P-Tex is made in one of two ways, extrusion or sintering, which we will define below.

To produce **extruded** bases, polyethylene is first heated, and then formed to the desired size by pressing it between rollers until it is a given width and thickness, usually around 85–92 millimeters wide and 1.2 millimeters thick, with a molecular weight of not more than 500,000. This process allows fast production of bases that will glide well, but will not accept a great deal of wax.

Continuing tests showed that bases with higher molecular weight had better glide characteristics. These bases were first tested for racing, but the results were equally important for the all-around skier: A ski that glides well is easier to turn, leading to more controlled skiing and greatly reduced energy demand.

To produce **sintered** bases, polyethylene powder—finely ground polyethylene—is placed in a press which can be heated and then cooled, and the powder is compressed into a cake. The round cake is taken out of the press and peeled on a machine resembling a lathe. The continuous "peel" is used to make ski bases. Because sintered bases have larger "pores," they absorb more wax, thus holding wax, and speed, longer.

Ski bases do not actually have "pores." The wax is absorbed into the "open," or "amorphous," area between the P-Tex particles, but we will continue to use the word "pore" for convenience, and because it is a useful mental image.

Double-sintered bases take the process one step further: the high molecular cakes formed in the sintering process are reground into 3-millimeter particles, then pressed and heated once again. This type of base (molecular weight 3,500,000 to 8,000,000) was said to demonstrate even higher wax absorption and retention, and to be less easily scratched. However, after a brief flurry, interest in this type of base faded. In my experience, skis with double-sintered bases weren't appreciably faster, and the often violently contrasting colors used made it virtually impossible to see what you were doing when waxing them or working on your bases.

## Graphite and Other Additives

Most racing skis now come with P-Tex 2000 and P-Tex 4000 bases, and almost all skis are now produced with black bases, henceforth referred to as the black electric base or "BEB." In BEB bases graphite and other additives help not only to reduce static electricity buildup, but also to produce a self-lubricating surface, again making for a faster ski. BEB bases have proven to be an advantage in a broad range of conditions.

Let's take a quick look at the effect of static buildup: As the ski glides over the snow, static electricity is generated, and the charged ski attracts dirt. By adding graphite, which is a conductor, to the P-Tex, which is not a conductor, an effort was made to ground the ski, and thus eliminate the positive static charge.

In addition, a process of electrolysis may occur, which may partly account for the "white" spots that show up on a worn black base. These white, or gray, spots are fibrils of P-Tex that have lost their graphite content. They can usually be brushed off, but their presence is also a valuable indicator of areas of unequal pressure distribution. They can be avoided by choosing skis with better pressure distribution, waxing with graphite wax, waxing more thoroughly, or by eliminating possible bumps and high spots.

Ski companies have done extensive research into what kind of base works best on what kind of snow, how much graphite to add to the base material, etc. Most ski bases come from the same one or two factories, but the ski manufacturers determine the precise "mix" that goes into their bases. For example, Cera F or similar fluorinated compounds have been introduced into some bases, and even Gallium has been tried. Such additives should make a better self-lubricated surface as wax wears off, and may help fluorocarbon "waxes" to adhere better. Base compounds are chosen for optimum performance on the projected snow type the ski is intended for, and are continually tested on snow and updated in production.

## What Base Type Do You Need?

The simplest—and most effective—way to deal with all these various base types is to buy skis that are designed for the conditions in which you plan to use them: powder/cold skis for cold conditions, klister/warm skis for metamorphosed snow, and so on.

Remember that a good ski is a good ski: a ski designed for warm conditions will sometimes be very good in cold conditions, and vice versa (though it is rarer for a cold-snow ski to be good in warm conditions). It pays to know your skis.

Now let's have a look at the one thing that determines how we approach everything from ski selection to wax application: the snow.

**Chapter**

# SNOW

A basic understanding of snow is important for developing techniques for getting the most out of your skis, and for evolving strategies for overcoming snow's tendency to slow skis through friction against the base of the ski.

## Characteristics of Snow

The most important characteristics of snow, vis-à-vis ski preparation, are water content, temperature of snow and air, size and shape of crystals, and dirt content. Snow varies in hardness, crystal size, and flexibility. This variation is what governs our choice of wax and base preparation.

Some kinds of snow, especially when temperatures are between about -1°C and -7°C, are very easy to glide or kick on; others, such as very cold snow, very wet snow, and snow around 0°C, are more difficult to deal with. Still others, notably dirty snow, make it hard to maintain glide at distances of over a few kilometers. Owing to industrial pollution, we are seeing more and more dirty snow wherever we go, so dirt resistance is an important factor in choosing a wax.

Let's have a look at the various kinds of snow, starting with the coldest.

### Extremely Cold Snow

At the bottom of the temperature range, extremely cold snow presents very specific problems for making a ski glide well. Generally, very cold snow will be characterized by sharp, pointed crystals, which, because of the cold, are also very inelastic. These sharp crystals bite into the wax on the base, like gravel into a tire, and retard glide; at the same time they are highly abrasive, causing rapid wax wear. For these reasons, cold snow requires a very smooth base and a very hard wax. It is easy to get good kick in cold snows, but, as with glide-waxing, finding a kick wax that glides and is "free" can be difficult.

### Cold and Medium Snow

Cold and medium-temperature snows are the easiest conditions for which to prepare skis. The crystal is not as sharp as with extremely cold snow, and thus does not penetrate as deeply or produce as much drag; the crystal structure is not so rigid, the crystal having become somewhat elastic. Both factors mean that this kind of snow produces less friction, while there is generally not enough water present to cause problems with suction and water dispersal. Virtually all wax manufacturers produce waxes that work well from around -1° to -7° or 8°C.

### Zero-Degree Snow

Snow around 0°C produces a whole set of nightmares peculiar unto itself. Higher amounts of water are usually present, and at the same time freezing is very close. Thus, suction is a problem, as is the chance of icing. Modern glide waxes (fluorocarbons) are at their best in this temperature range, and even in kick wax, the new waxes, many of them containing fluorocarbons, are more effective than was previously the case. "Mechanical" kick is also a possible solution ("fish scales," "hairies," etc.).

### Above Zero Degrees

Temperatures above freezing (air temperature, that is; snow can never go above 0°C, or it ceases to be snow) mean three things:

1. Large amounts of water are likely to be present. Suction-induced drag is caused by excess water but can be minimized by aggressive base structure and application of fluorocarbons (henceforth "fluoros") or "fluoroparaffins" to lower surface tension. "Fluoroparaffins" are waxes with greater or lesser concentrations of fluorocarbons in them, as opposed to "straight" fluorocarbons, which come in the form of powders or solid cakes. (For a thorough discussion of fluorocarbons, see Chapter 13.)

2. The snow crystal will have metamorphosed into a

larger, rounder structure through melting and refreez-
ing. As snow crystals become rounder, we need softer
waxes for both kick (klisters) and glide, in order to
make it possible for the crystal to penetrate the wax.

3. Dirt is likely to be increasingly present as evaporation
occurs; more on this in the next section.

### Special Considerations

In addition to temperature and water content, there are two
other factors that greatly affect the functioning of the ski and the
wax: dirt and "grooming."

**Dirt.** Owing to increasing pollution, there is more and more
dirt present in most snows. In addition, as snow evaporates or
melts, the dirt already present in the snow becomes more and
more concentrated in the remaining snow.

Dirt causes abrasion of the wax; it causes friction by imbed-
ding itself in the wax; and it causes more suction by clogging
structure. Kick waxes pick up dirt and create drag at an alarming
rate, as well as mixing with dirt to form a harder outer layer, thus
making for reduced kick as the snow finds it more difficult to bite
into the wax.

While softer waxes may be best for matching wax hardness
to crystal size in wet, warm conditions, harder waxes would
seem to be indicated for dirt resistance. Soft glide waxes, perhaps containing silicone or Teflon, will work very well for short
distances. However, pure fluoros will usually be an advantage
in these conditions, especially over longer distances, owing to
their ability to resist dirt. Most manufacturers are also producing fluorinated kick waxes (see Chapter 13) and klisters for moist
snow, for all of the same reasons: less friction and increased dirt
resistance.

**Grooming and "aging" of snow.** New snow has the most
pointed crystals. Grooming "ages" the snow and causes it to lose
its sharpness, as well as mixes it, creating more uniform conditions along the track.

Here's how the "aging" process occurs: The snow is simply
knocked around, and the points break off the crystals. Grooming "sinters" the snow as well, taking the air out of it and allowing it to compress more.

The knocking-around also causes minute, peripheral melting, which in turn encourages the crystals either to lose sharpness or to bond together as they refreeze, making the snow both less aggressive and also firmer. This, too, has the happy effect of tending to make the snow more uniform around the course.

Because groomed snow is more "rounded," a softer wax, for both kick and glide, may be indicated. Note that because groomed snow is firmer, owing to sintering and melting/refreezing, it can also be more abrasive.

## Types of Snow

In the early 1990s, we developed a schematic of snow types and conditions in an effort to describe conditions as closely as possible for our records (see Appendix 3). These categories will perhaps seem overly complex for the citizen racer, and it is certainly not necessary to use all of them in order to produce fast skis, but by way of illustration of how many snow types there are, I'd like to include the following schematic:

| Snow Type | Condition |
|---|---|
| New: | Dry, windblown, glazed, damp, saturated |
| Fine: | Packed, moist, saturated |
| Coarse: | Hard, moist, sugar, saturated |
| Man-made: | Hard, packed, moist, sugar, saturated |

Now let's have a look at the theory of waxing in more depth: what do waxes do, and why do they work, and sometimes, why don't they work?

**Chapter**

# HOW KICK WAX WORKS

There is always a great deal of fuss about glide wax, but it's a good thing to remember that in a race, in training, and even on a tour, we tend to spend the greater part of our time—up to 70 percent—climbing. In the case of skating, this is certainly helped by the good glide we can get from applying the right glide wax. But when it comes to classic skiing, I think we worry too much about the wrong thing, and neglect the single most important factor in a successful workout or a good tour: the kick wax.

Later, we'll talk at length about the application of kick waxes, but for now it's a good idea to have an overview of how they work.

The function of a kick wax is to allow snow crystals to penetrate more deeply into the wax than is the case with glide waxes. This penetration "nails" the ski to the snow, giving the skier traction and allowing him or her to move forward. The analogy of a rubber-soled shoe on a bed of nails is appropriate.

This simple picture is made more complex by the fact that kick waxes must also be able to glide when under less pressure, as when the kick has ended and the glide begins. Glide is reinforced by mechanical means, that is, the camber of the ski, which lifts the kick wax off the snow as we glide. The stiffness of the ski, the length of the wax pocket, and the weight and strength of the individual skier are also factors.

## The Right Kick Wax for the Situation

The type and condition of the snow determines which kick wax we will use, so let's have a brief look at how different snows affect the choice of wax for classic skiing.

### Type of Snow

**New, hard, pointed snows** call for hard waxes, such as a green.

**Groomed snow,** which has become softer, more blunt, and more tightly packed, will call for a softer wax, say a violet.

**Metamorphosed snow,** which has thawed and refrozen into larger, rounder particles, requires an even softer wax for the broad "points" of the crystal to penetrate. When the points are even broader, as in ice or slush, a klister, very soft indeed, is needed.

### Icing

To further complicate the picture, kick waxes can "freeze" and chip off if used below their temperature range. Or if crystals penetrate too deeply, ice will rapidly build up. The same thing can happen when there is water present but the temperature is below freezing, such as in falling snow just below 0°C. The result in either situation is that the skier has either no kick at all or is carrying several pounds of snow around under his feet, and not getting any glide.

Because it is sometimes unclear around the freezing point whether klister or hard wax will be best, and because water is apt to be present at this temperature, wax choice in this range can be a nightmare. (It is equally difficult to hit the right glide wax at 0°C, but because the effect of a miss is less spectacular, kick-waxing gets all the publicity.) Still, new kick waxes are being developed which deal fairly effectively with zero-degree conditions, and some of the universal or multigrade waxes work well across a broad range of conditions, as do a number of new fluorinated kick waxes.

A good rule of thumb, which we will discuss in greater depth in Chapter 12, is to avoid klister if at all possible. This will help with the icing problem, and will often produce a faster ski.

### Dirt Again

Kick waxes pick up a great deal of dirt, owing to their relative softness, and to the fact that they stop and are pressed against the snow at the moment of kick (try double-poling through obvious patches of dirt). This dirt limits the effectiveness of the wax by (1) creating drag (and abrasion), (2) hardening the wax, and (3) limiting the available wax surface: too many pine needles, for example, simply reduce the amount of surface wax available for the snow to penetrate.

Softer kick waxes will also migrate back along the glide surface, thus slowing glide by merely being there; this is a particular problem with klisters.

A stiffer ski may help to avoid wax/snow drag, as well as some degree of dirt pickup.

New kick waxes and klisters are being developed which contain many different additives: fluorocarbons, graphite, and so on. The idea is to create a wax/klister that will glide better when the kick phase is finished, and will resist dirt, all without diminishing effective kick. Early examples of these waxes met with variable success—some did not feel freer, kick was compromised, or the waxes wore off fast (although alternating layers of tar-based wax and a graphite-impregnated wax does produce very free skis in some new-snow conditions).

The new generation of waxes, however, are extremely effective. They really are faster and freer, and because of new formulations they also offer better kick over a wider range of temperatures, and adhere well to the base. There has indeed been progress!

Because kick waxes can produce so much drag if used wrongly and/or when dirt is present, and because lack of kick makes an effective stride impossible, testing for the right kick wax is far more important than testing for glide wax, especially if conditions are changing. When in doubt, go for "close enough" with glide, but take care of kick.

Now let's take a look at glide waxes.

**Chapter**

# HOW GLIDE WAX WORKS

The purpose of this chapter is to give an overview of two things: what glide wax does, and what kinds there are. I am not a chemist; my intent is simply to provide a practical system of understanding and directing the application of glide waxes.

For the recreational skier, almost the right glide wax will probably be good enough (kick wax is another story). For a well-trained skier with good technique, however, who has the proper skis for his or her weight, ability, and the snow, more careful applications will make a significant difference in ski performance.

To understand how to use glide wax effectively and easily, let's take a look at the various theories of how and why wax works. Although they are not fact (no one has ever actually seen the surface of the snow interacting with a ski base and wax), these theories all seem to work and are helpful tools for envisioning what goes on when a ski comes into contact with the snow. The four theories involve crystal elasticity, controlled friction/wet lubrication, surface tension and dry lubrication, and dirt repulsion.

## Crystal Elasticity

This theory has not seen much attention but is worth a short discussion nonetheless. According to the crystal elasticity theory, a ski glides when the snow crystal bends or collapses. Colder snow crystals are less elastic, so the wax needs to be stronger in order to hold and bend the crystal. The warmer the snow, the easier it is to bend the crystal, and the softer the wax has to be to allow sufficient penetration and grip on the crystal.

I am not aware of any work being done with this theory, but it does help us visualize what goes on when skis are dragging, especially in very cold weather or with new, sharp snow.

## Controlled Friction

This is the classic theory, which holds that if we create a controlled amount of friction between the ski base and the snow, we can melt just enough snow so that we can glide on a minute layer of water droplets, which act not unlike tiny ball bearings. By suiting the hardness of the wax to the characteristics of the snow crystal, an ideal degree of penetration of the crystal into the wax will occur. This will produce controlled friction, which in turn causes peripheral melting of the snow crystal (a very small amount of melting, just at the edges of the crystal). The ski then glides on a very thin layer of water droplets. For this wet lubrication, the ideal wax for the given snow is determined by:

- the shape of the snow crystal (its pointedness)
- the temperature of the snow (a colder snow will need more heat/friction to produce melting)
- the strength of the snow (a cold crystal being stronger than a warmer one)
- the moisture present (we do not want to produce too much water, or we will get a suction effect)

The controlled friction theory produces observable and predictable results, and this makes it useful for practical application.

To expand on this theory, a too-hard wax will not allow penetration by the crystal, and there will be too little friction to produce the desired water film. (This is further complicated by the effect of the skier's weight.) At the same time, a too-soft wax will allow too much penetration, which will produce too much friction, creating too much water. An even softer wax would allow the crystals to penetrate the wax so much that motion would not be possible, something like stepping on the aforementioned bed of nails with a rubber-soled shoe. Softer waxes will also collect dirt more readily.

Let's take a look at how the theory works in some specific conditions:

**Cold snows** present special difficulties. Because very cold crystals tend to be either very pointed, or very stiff, or both, it takes a good deal of power to create the right amount of friction to melt the crystal. It also takes a good deal of heat to cause melting at low temperatures, and it is very difficult to avoid drag. This is why cold snows tend to be slow, and why really good cold-snow waxes are both hard, and hard to find. At this point, dry lubrication becomes an issue. We will look at dry lubrication later on in this chapter.

**Grooming** also has an effect on glide. Since grooming knocks the points off the crystals, it will facilitate getting a good glide at cold temperatures. At the same time, however, grooming fuses the rigid crystals of cold snow together, and cold groomed snow can be very abrasive; waxes tend to wear off fast in these conditions. This is another reason why hard, durable waxes are important in cold conditions.

**New snow** partakes of some of the characteristics of cold snow. As it has not been groomed, and thus the crystals have not been "de-pointed," there tends to be more friction.

**Medium-temperature snows** are easier to wax for. The crystals are less pointed and less rigid, and usually there is already some water present (but not enough to create significant suction), and so it is easier to achieve good glide in medium conditions. This is why good medium-temperature waxes are so plentiful.

**Warm snows** tend to be wetter and to have duller crystals. For this reason, warm/wet snow waxes are softer (to allow penetration). At the same time, as more water is present, more suction is likely to occur, and the ski slows. At this point, structure—small grooves that are pressed or cut into the base of the ski to relieve suction—may become vital in order to relieve the drag caused by suction. (We'll examine structure in Chapter 9.) The surface tension of the wax, which affects the shape and size of the water droplet, also becomes a factor.

In addition, melting will usually have increased the amount of dirt present in the snow. There are fewer good waxes available for these particular conditions; various additives and alternatives (such as fluorocarbons) may be effective.

## Surface Tension

Once the water layer has formed, it is necessary to control the shape and size of the droplets. This is done partly by controlling the amount of friction, and hence the amount of water. However, different wax ingredients help control the size and shape of the droplets by varying the amount of surface tension.

Much the same way that raindrops form differently on a freshly waxed car, "beading up," various types of waxes affect the size and shape of the water droplets. A large, wide droplet will produce suction, while a smaller, rounder one will act more as a lubricant/bearing.

Surface tension helps to explain why different waxes, supposedly for the same conditions, will act quite differently; and also why a given wax will produce different results under only slightly different conditions, such as in different areas or countries, where, say, the water content of the snow may be different at the same temperature.

The most obvious example of the application of this theory is fluorocarbon "wax." Fluorocarbons (fluoros) have a much higher surface tension than normal paraffins, as well as a lower coefficient of friction. The result is that a much smaller, rounder "bead" forms on a fluorocarbon-treated ski base than on a normal wax. This is the main reason why fluorocarbon "waxes" function best in high humidity. (The other reason is that moister snow, especially snow where melting is occurring, tends to have a higher dirt content, and fluorocarbons are very dirt resistant.)

Fluorocarbons work over a very broad temperature range, and over a fairly broad humidity range. They are at their best in high humidity, and the higher the humidity, the broader the temperature range: I have used fluorocarbons as low as -13°C, with great success, if humidity was sufficiently high.

But fluorocarbons will not always test the fastest. Often their real advantage will not "kick in" until quite a few kilometers have been skied. At this point, the fluoros will still be going fast, owing to their dirt resistance and general toughness, while paraffins have slowed down. Thus, fluoros can be classed as a long-distance "wax," and sometimes not appropriate for shorter distances, such as junior races. A more extensive discussion of fluoros will follow in Chapters 12 and 13.

## Dry Lubrication and Additives

The idea here is much the same as in "ordinary" lubrication: the friction between two surfaces is reduced by adding lubricating agents such as Teflon, graphite, molybdenum, graphite, or silicone. Dry lubrication plays a part in waxing for all kinds of snow, dry or wet. Additives alter the surface tension of the wax, and can affect wear.

In colder snow, where wet lubrication is more difficult to achieve, additives such as graphite will produce the needed lubrication. This is also the case in drier snow.

In addition, some manufacturers claim that the addition of graphite, molybdenum, etc., makes a wax (or a base) more conductive, thus allowing the ski to "dump" static electric buildups, which attract dirt.

Many skiers prefer to use a graphite wax as a travel wax, to protect the ski during transport, on the theory that this helps to maintain the graphite level in the base. Manufacturers differ on the application of graphite waxes, some using them as base waxes, some as mixers, some as overlayers, and some simply as a premixed wax for use in specific conditions. Particle size also varies from brand to brand, affecting penetration.

Recent experience also leads me to believe that maintaining a level of fluorocarbon content in bases may be an advantage, at least for warmer-snow skis. Thus fluoro-graphite waxes may be the perfect wax for protection during travel and storage. With these in the base, you will be maintaining the graphite and fluoro level of the base, and you will be one stage closer to final waxing: scrape, add the wax of the day, go.

Parenthetically, both of the above theories (dry lubrication and "dumping" static charges) are cited in reference to the superior performance of graphite bases under some conditions.

Glide paraffins with graphite added are often at their best in either dirty conditions or in low humidity, owing to their anti-static properties. At the same time, graphites, etc., because of their antistatic characteristics, may also decrease dirt buildup in wet snows. Read what it says on the box!

In my experience, graphite-type additives and/or sublayers can dramatically reduce wear, thus prolonging good glide. If asked for a rule of thumb, I would say that when in doubt, use an additive or sublayer. This can improve glide and wear characteristics, and only rarely will have a significantly negative effect on glide.

Silicone is a wet-snow additive, and many companies produce either silicone gel or liquid, or silicone additives (paraffins with silicone already mixed in). Silicones function well in wet snow and very badly in dry snow, and many feel that they are given to picking up dirt—so perhaps their application should be limited to shorter races.

The 1995 World Championship in Thunder Bay, Ontario, was the scene of some bizarre—and effective—solutions to an unbelievably high dirt content. Before the skate legs of the pursuit races, skiers were coming in after 5 kilometers with black skis, and running a scraper down the base of a ski would yield a tablespoon of sticky black scum. Skis were dirtying so fast that halfway through a 5-kilometer training run, skiers were having to skate downhills and V1 flats.

Cleaning skis thus became a major priority, which all the teams solved by placing cleaning boards across the trail—boards wrapped in toweling or Fibertex soaked with various cleaning agents from wax remover to (yes, really!) Gunk. Skiers would pass over these boards to clean their skis, greatly increasing glide in the process. But the really "out there" stuff was the "wax": while most teams used various forms of fluorocarbons, Austria used diesel oil on their boards. The Slovene team, for which I was doing service, used two-cycle oil at Matej Soklic's suggestion. It worked!

The oils were the only thing we could find that stayed clean and kept moving. The moral: Keep your mind open, and keep experimenting!

## Dirt Repulsion

A few more words about dirt repulsion/resistance are in order. This is an area that grows more important all the time, as more and more snow shows pollution. Dirty snow is not limited to industrial areas. Spring snow is usually dirty, as is snow in any melting condition: as the snow evaporates or melts, it leaves behind dirt in greater and greater concentrations. Dirt is also present in areas with trees, as falling leaves and needles carry dirt or add themselves to the mix, and dust blows off trees onto the snow.

Dirt repulsion is an important consideration in selecting the best wax. A clean ski will be faster, and a ski that stays clean will remain fast longer. The following should be kept in mind:

- A harder wax will resist dirt better than a softer one at a given temperature.
- *Prolonged* good glide can be more important than *immediate* good glide. A wax that is perhaps a little slower when initially tested may be going fast 50 or more kilometers later because of dirt resistance and resistance to wear, while another wax, perhaps faster initially, will pick up more dirt and/or wear off. Some waxes are good for short races only, and some will be better in longer races.
- It is always a good idea to retest a wax after it has been "skied in," to check on slow-down. When we were in full swing with the U.S. Cross-Country Team, and had enough staff, we would test eight or even sixteen or more waxes, then take the best two or three test skis (depending on how many skiers were available) and "ski them in" for at least 5 kilometers before retesting. Often the number two or number three wax would be faster after doing some distance, and these would be the waxes we would use for racing.

Now we have a good understanding of how to choose effective skis. We have examined the materials they are made of, and the environment we expect them to perform in. At this point, it's time to move on to tools and techniques needed for preparing the skis for optimal performance.

# Part 2

# TECHNIQUES OF SKI PREPARATION

This next part of the book will address the techniques and tools that are necessary for effective preparation of skis. Here is where the "hands on" work begins.

For this you will need some basic tools: a good steel scraper, a sharp plastic scraper, a good waxing iron, some brushes, and a form bench. The proper use of each of these tools will be discussed in subsequent chapters as we go over each stage of ski preparation, from flattening the base through wax application and final polishing.

The stages of ski preparation form a logical continuum. To do the best job possible, we need to understand why we are doing each procedure, so we'll begin by asking a fundamental question: "What makes a ski slow?" Each succeeding chapter of Part 2 will be aimed at learning how to use a tool or apply a technique that will allow a ski to function properly.

**Chapter**

# WHAT MAKES A SKI SLOW?

*An object will persist in its velocity*
*until affected by outside forces.*
—law of physics

I always work on the assumption that a ski wants to go fast. So what slows it down? If we understand the forces that slow a ski, we have taken a solid step toward learning how to make it go fast—and to keep it going fast. Below is a list of the "forces" that slow a ski, in descending order of importance. Please note that this is a working order; a *really* wrong wax, for example, will move wax way up the list.

1. Inadequate technique (the best skis in the world will not make up for poor technique)
2. The wrong flex—pressure distribution not suited to the skier or to specific conditions
3. The wrong base structure for the conditions
4. Base in poor condition
5. The wrong wax for the conditions
6. Poor or improper final prepping
7. The wrong base type

## Flex

We discussed choosing a ski with the proper flex in Chapter 1, but we did not go into how flex affects glide. If a ski has the wrong flex, it will plow or "wallow": if it is too stiff, only the tip and tail will put pressure against the snow, causing the ski to "plow" its way through the snow; or, if the ski is too soft, only the middle section will exert pressure against the snow, and the ski will "wallow" and be unstable. Pressure distribution relates to the skier's weight and to the hardness/softness of the track (and is why different skis are needed for different conditions) as well as to the overall design and construction of the ski.

The need for proper pressure distribution is equally important in both classic and skating techniques, although the proper distribution is different in both cases because the different techniques put different mechanical demands on the skis.

In the case of skating skis, a more or less even pressure distribution over the entire length of the ski is the starting point. In contrast to gliding with the weight equally distributed on both skis, as in a downhill run, pressure distribution is very different in skating when putting one's full weight on one ski in gliding after the "kick," and with several times one's body weight on the ski during the push-off.

With classic skis, proper flex allows a kick wax to contact the snow during the kick but keeps it *off* the snow so it won't drag during glide. At the same time, the flex has to allow relatively even ski/snow pressure in the glide areas; this calls for a very different pressure distribution than in the case of a skating ski.

Further, too stiff a classic ski will make the ski hard to run uphill on, and may require a change in technique, as well as tire the skier earlier.

## Base Structure

As we have seen, a ski glides on a thin film of water. Too much water can cause suction, which slows the ski. To eliminate suction, we **structure** the base, adding rills (small grooves cut or pressed into the base of the ski to relieve suction) or creating structure through wire-brushing or stone-grinding (see Chapter 9).

A useful analogy is that of putting two plates of glass together. The plates will be very hard to pull apart unless we put some kind of air channels on the glass, or add holes to allow the suction to dissipate.

Structure is very important. No structure at all can make for very bad skis, but please note that for all practical purposes, *almost* the right structure is as good as the right structure. Always use structure, but don't worry too much about which type.

## Base Condition

A fast pair of skis will usually keep their speed even with a lot of dings and scratches. Skis stand up to a good deal more abuse than might be thought. Some people, and I am one of them, spend far too much time trying to keep bases perfectly pristine. Better to maintain an attitude of "Let's get out there and ski." Stop worrying, keep it simple, and go find some snow!

"Hair" on a base, on the other hand, slows a ski considerably. "Hair" consists of small fibers of base material caused by factory sanding or grinding. Recently, however, manufacturers are doing a better job, and "factory hair" is more or less a thing of the past. Still, hair can be raised by sanding, by grinding, by accident, and even by Fibertexing. Aside from deliberate structure, a base should be as smooth as possible.

The two most common kinds of base damage are caused by poor scraping, scraping with a dull scraper ("chatter" or "orange skin"), or by ironing too hot and melting the base material ("sealed base").

Large scratches, bumps, and other defects are also a concern and can often be repaired (see Chapter 18), but in nine cases out of ten they need not cause overly great concern.

## Wax

A very bad glide wax will slow the ski considerably, but as with structure, *almost* the right glide wax is usually good enough. Skiers tend to spend too much energy looking for the magic wax. There isn't any. But with modern waxes growing better and better, and working well over a broader and broader range of conditions, it is relatively easy to find a good wax for almost all conditions.

Kick wax is another issue. "The music plays on the uphills." A slippery kick wax will tire the skier quickly, will make getting up the hills difficult or impossible, and will quickly have a bad effect on technique. At the same time, a kick wax that grabs or drags can have an equally negative effect on performance. Luckily, as was the case with glide waxes, modern technology makes finding a good wax easier than used to be the case, and improved track grooming has had the same effect. Ultimately, the skier has to *make* it work.

## Final Prepping

Improper final prepping of the base can slow a ski. Be careful of the following:

**Thorough scraping and/or brushing is extremely important.** Leaving too much wax on the base will cause drag, and/or pick up dirt.

**Not allowing the ski to cool can cause icing,** especially with kick waxes (where it can also make some kinds of layering impossible). In the case of very hard waxes, scraping too cool can impair performance.

**Poor corking can cause lumpy kick wax,** which will cause drag and limit kick. Kick wax gives grip when the points of the snow crystals penetrate the wax: it does *not* work like a snow tread, where the more aggressive the pattern, the better the traction. This is why we do not stud or chain skis. This is also why patterned no-wax skis are almost always slower than waxed skis (though in rare conditions around 0°C it's better to have some kick, as opposed to too much!).

## Base Types

Most companies offer skis with "powder" or "cold" bases, or "klister" or "warm" bases, etc. Much research has shown that certain types of bases are better suited to certain types of snow, as we have seen in Chapters 2 and 3. Additives in the base material also have an effect.

As a general rule, simply follow the guidelines provided by the manufacturer, but at the same time, experience has shown that a warm base ski may sometimes be faster in cold snow, or vice versa. It pays to know your skis.

Flex (covered in Chapter 1) is the single most important factor in determining the speed of a ski.

We are now ready to start using the tools we need to prepare our skis. The single most useful tool in the box is the scraper, so let's begin practical application of all we've discussed by learning how to use the metal scraper.

**Chapter**

# THE SCRAPER

One of the two most important tools for ski preparation is a *good* steel scraper (the other is the cork, discussed in Chapter 12). The scraper is the simplest and fastest tool for base reconditioning that you have, and will quickly become your most trusted "diagnostic tool": the feel of a steel scraper against a ski base tells more about the condition of the base than anything else I know. The scraper is also probably the most misused and the least understood of tools—and the hardest to find. For these reasons, we will devote a chapter especially to the use of the scraper.

A good steel scraper is one small enough to use handily, stiff enough not to bend, thin enough to sharpen easily, and hard enough to take a good edge, and to keep it. The best scrapers I have seen are the cobalt steel scrapers. These are exactly the right shape and size, unbendable, and made of an extremely hard steel. Mine is now almost a decade old and my most valued and well-traveled tool. (Use of a plastic scraper, for removing wax, will be discussed in Chapter 11.)

You will also need to have a good form bench to work on, one that will support the ski over its entire length. A "point support" vise system, supporting only the middle, tip, and tail of the ski, will not allow you to apply enough pressure with your tools, and some portable or collapsible benches will damage the top layer of the ski if you are being sufficiently energetic.

## When to Steel-Scrape

I prefer to apply structure to a smooth base, and as it is often a good idea to take off the outer layer of oxidized P-Tex for better wax penetration, I steel-scrape skis pretty frequently. You can also steel-scrape skis in order to flatten them; we will cover flattening in Chapter 8.

Bases can be sealed through ironing at too high a temperature; this will close the pores by partially melting the base. (Bases melt in the neighborhood of 130–135°C; I usually wax at 100°, and rarely over 115°. Be sure your iron has a good temperature control!) Careless factory grinding can also be a frequent source of too much heat. Careless use of wax-removal chemicals can often leave a film, clogging the pores and/or drying out the base. Base material also degenerates through an accumulation of dirt in storage and travel, and is negatively affected by direct sunlight and oxygen.

It's a good idea to **open the base**, by removing "aged" P-Tex. This opens the "pore" structure (that is, the amorphous space between the solid bits of P-Tex that absorb the wax) and assures better wax penetration.

I steel-scrape skis to get down to clean, new plastic two or three times a year, when the texture has to be removed or changed, or when the base has become less than smooth. It is not necessary to remove a great deal of base, and you can do a good deal of gentle scraping; I lightly steel-scrape test skis between every waxing, and some pairs have gone through several seasons of this, without any visible sign of losing too much base. Beware of scraping too much; a thorough job removes just enough material to achieve smoothness. Given sensitive scraping and gentle use, a base should still last quite a few seasons.

(It is impossible to predict just how long a base will last; this is the product of initial base thickness, which varies; how much has to be taken off if a base has to be flattened; and whether base thickness is uniform. Shallow and/or narrow grooves are an indication that the useful life of a ski is about over, but there are no rules.)

## Sharpening and Maintaining the Scraper

To sharpen the scraper, a good, flat stone is needed, about 6 inches long. Most sharpening stones tend to develop a groove or to get out of flat. Diamond stones will not do this, and, in addition, they are hard enough to sharpen a cobalt scraper. I prefer the medium-sized diamond stone, roughly 6 by 2 inches, and find the blue, or medium "grit" the most useful. I have also used the black, or coarse stone, but this can produce a bad burr if not used very carefully. *Do not use this stone to sharpen carbide pole tips*, such as those used for roller skiing on pavement—reserve it for scrapers only. Use your stone wet, and wipe or rinse the stone clean afterwards. Dry the stone, and keep it in its case.

Diamond stones wear very slowly, but they do "fill," which makes them feel worn out. To rejuvenate a diamond stone, scrub vigorously with a stiff brush and an abrasive commercial scrubbing powder such as Comet or Ajax. If there is much wax present, use hot water with the scrubbing powder. Wax can be removed from a stone by scrubbing with wax remover.

It is *very important* to have a good, 90° edge on the scraper. To achieve this, take two steps:

1. Place the scraper flat on the stone, and move it backwards and forwards to make it perfectly square and to remove any "burr" or "wire edge."

2. Place a block of wood on the stone, using this as a guide for the scraper (figure 4) and to keep the scraper at a 90° angle to the stone. Move the scraper backwards and forwards, being sure not to let it or the block slip sideways, which can create a pronounced burr. In the case of a new scraper, this may take a good deal of work.

*Figure 4. Sharpening a steel scraper. Note the use of the wood block to ensure a 90-degree edge. The "stone" is a diamond stone.*

*Figure 5. Steel scraping a base. Note the width of the peel being raised, as well as the angle of the scraper to the base: it's as close to 90-degrees as I can manage. Note also the fingers at the side of the ski, acting as guides.*

A great deal of pressure is not needed. Be sure to use water on the stone.

These two steps are necessary to create a 90° edge on the scraper. I prefer to use a 90° edge, as opposed to a burred edge. A really sharp 90° will cut spectacularly, and a properly sharpened scraper will "peel" a ski in just a few passes. The peelings should resemble Scotch tape: they should be quite wide, up to the entire width of the area being scraped, and it should be possible to create a handful in three or four passes (see figure 5).

Some service people prefer a thinner scraper, with a pronounced burr, because burred scrapers remove base very quickly and are quick to sharpen. If you prefer to use a thin scraper, I recommend stiffening it by backing it with a cork or a piece of wood; otherwise, bending the scraper can result in a concave or convex base. However, a burred edge can be hard to control, can leave structure in the base, and is very easy to overuse to the point of damaging the base.

To put a burr on a scraper, start by creating a 90° edge, as above. When this is done, clamp the scraper in a vise. Now pull a burr onto

*Figure 6. Burnishing the edge of a steel scraper with a burnishing tool. Hold the scraper tightly in a vice, then "roll" a wire edge, or "burr" over. Note that I prefer simply to use a 90-degree edge.*

the edge by drawing a hardened steel burnishing tool along the edge, as shown (figure 6). Any piece of steel will work as a burnisher—I have used a screwdriver—but a hardened round or triangular tool will do the job best. Burnishers can sometimes be found in good woodworking shops (also a good source for the thinner kind of scraper) or can be ordered from specialty tool catalogs.

Caution! More damage is done to ski bases by dull or improperly sharpened scrapers than by anything else, except a too-hot iron. Proper sharpening is of the utmost importance, not only for the good of the base and the proper function of the skis, but also for the effective use of the scraper. It takes time and experimentation to put a proper edge on a scraper, but once this is mastered, there is very little that can't be done with a scraper in terms of flattening a base, exposing fresh P-Tex, and eliminating slight scratches.

A plastic scraper should be treated much the same way as a steel scraper, and kept sharp at all times; but as plastic scrapers are used only for wax removal, we will discuss them in Chapter 11, under "Scraping."

## How to Use the Scraper

Be prepared to use strong motions with your scraper; this takes thumb and arm strength, and it takes time to develop a feel for what is happening when scraping. The scraper cuts best at almost a 90° angle to the ski base (refer back to figure 5); the more acute the angle, the more you are just pressing, and the less you are presenting a cutting edge to the base.

Guide the scraper with a finger on each side of the ski—a slip to the side can do a *lot* of nasty and undesired cutting, if the scraper is properly sharp. (And if it isn't, you shouldn't be using it!)

If there is a great deal of work to be done, or if the base is hardened as the result of heat generated when grinding or by using too hot an iron, heavy strokes should do the job. If the base is unyielding, I sometimes resharpen the scraper with a black/coarse stone, to put a slight burr on the edge; this will cut through almost anything. If the base is exceptionally hard to cut into, a few passes with 80- to 100-grit sandpaper can be used to break through a "crust."

After a while you will develop a feel for scraping. You will notice that after a few strokes the base of the ski will feel softer and more even; this means you are through the "crust" and into good base. With new skis and with badly oxidized skis, the first few passes will feel "scratchy" or like scraping a slate. Continue to scrape until this feeling changes to smooth and soft.

You can modify the scraping process with new skis if you are not confident in your scraping: wax, then scrape very gently, repeating the process until scraping feels even and soft.

You can follow up steel-scraping with a buffing pad, whether by hand or with a roto tool.

For finishing, use *quick, very light* strokes. This will yield what looks like dust, and will give you a very smooth finish. A base should look silky and have a deep glow to it.

Whenever you scrape, keep moving down the length of the ski, in order to avoid building up excess heat; work along the base to the tail, then go back to the tip again, and so on.

## Other Uses of the Scraper

**To flatten bumps or waves in the ski.** For this it is often a good idea to angle the scraper first one way, then the other, in relation to the direction of travel (figure 7). This avoids following the "waves" along the base of the ski, and several passes will remove high spots.

**To flatten skis that are convex or concave in the shovel** (where the tip curves upwards) **or tail.** Scraping can lessen the warp if it is not too great. Much warp is annoying but usually impossible to remove completely, and probably not very important, anyway, as these are areas of minimal pressure against the snow.

**To repair damaged edges.** Run the scraper very lightly down the edge of the skis at as close to 90° from the horizontal as possible. If a bit of jagged base is too much for the scraper, use a bit of sandpaper, and finish with a 3M Heavy Duty Stripping Pad, but be aware that sanding can produce a rounded edge, which may slip out when skating on very hard or icy tracks. One more note about edges: a rounded edge is desirable in the tip and tail area, as this will prevent the ski from "grabbing" too aggressively.

**To remove "orange skin"** (chatter caused by poor scraping and/or a too-hard base). Use *very light, quick* passes of a sharp scraper, or thoroughly rescrape with a good, sharp scraper. If this doesn't work, orange skin and chatter can be sanded out, but I

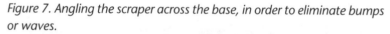

*Figure 7. Angling the scraper across the base, in order to eliminate bumps or waves.*

prefer not to use sandpaper on bases unless absolutely necessary, as sanding creates a great deal of "hair."

**To scrape new bases.** Bases have often been hardened by poor grinding, and/or have picked up dirt by sitting around the factory and store. Scraping can remove the factory texture, but new texture can be put in. Only do this if (a) you are very confident in your scraping, and (b) you are sure it is needed.

After steel-scraping, it is *very important* to reimpregnate the ski with paraffin. Use yellow or orange paraffins, as these softer waxes penetrate well, and be prepared to do a lot of ironing, adding more wax as needed. Finish with a wax close to the temperature of anticipated use.

Try to avoid steel-scraping shortly before a race: if the ski base is not properly resoaked, it may well lose all wax during the race.

Steel-scraping is a hard-learned and elusive art. There is little damage you can do to a ski that can't be repaired, but perhaps early efforts are best done on an old pair (or somebody else's skis). Practice scraping, experiment, be bold, and *always use a sharp scraper.*

A final word: Sanding can also be used for all of the operations described above. There are no disadvantages to sanding as far as the final result is concerned, but sanding does take much more time than scraping. Sanding will be covered in Chapter 8, but as sanding is much "safer," it may be the advisable method for those not comfortable with a steel scraper, and/or for juniors.

Now that we know how to sharpen and use a steel scraper, let's move on to the process of flattening and smoothing the ski base.

**Chapter**

# FLATTENING AND SMOOTHING THE BASE

A flat, smooth base provides the "platform" for good skiing. If the base of your ski is flat, it will glide better, be easier to wax, and even make it easier for you to balance. A smooth base—one with no hair, etc.—will be faster. So let's have a look at flattening and smoothing the base of our skis, the first and most basic step in preparing them for use. By doing so we will eliminate high and low spots; remove "aged" P-Tex and expose good, "open" base; and remove any "hair."

Flattening and smoothing the base is usually accomplished in the same operation, but we need to make a distinction between the two terms.

**Smoothing the base** refers to taking out scratches, small bumps, perhaps structure, hair, or orange skin.

**Flattening the base** refers to taking out waves, warps, bumps, and other irregularities, which can get into the base in a number of ways:

- through poor scraping or grinding (waves)
- through structural design (skis with round, "pressed" grooves are almost always slightly concave toward the center of the ski)
- through manufacturing (concave/convex tips and tails)
- through general maltreatment (bumps, dents)

If any of these various defects are extreme, they will hinder glide and result in a ski that is hard to structure, wax, or scrape. Flattening the base will also make the ski more stable, and will assure even pressure distribution and thus more even wax wear.

To check for flatness, hold a flat edge, such as a scraper, across the base every few inches, and sight down the length of the base to see if there is light under the scraper. There are also "true bars" for doing this, usually in the form of steel rods, which are easy simply to roll along the base.

Some skis can become warped and/or swollen because of the heat used in applying wax. This is probably unavoidable, as it is a function of structural design, and it will be very evident as you iron the ski, or as you scrape it afterwards. You can try to remove this kind of warp, but if the warp is too extreme, it is probably best ignored: you can take off too much base, and in extreme cases you run the risk of going through the base into core material.

There are three ways of flattening and/or smoothing bases; all three also open the base. In order of simplicity, these are: steel-scraping, sanding, and stone-grinding. Whichever method you use, remember that any process that removes base material is also "drying out" the base of your ski. *Always* finish any scraping, grinding, or sanding process with a thorough rewaxing!

## Steel-Scraping

We discussed the techniques of steel-scraping in the last chapter. This is the best and most expedient method readily available of preparing bases, and does not require a great deal of equipment. Given a sharp scraper, it leaves a flat, smooth base with no "hair."

This method does call for some caution, however: Steel-scraping requires considerable practice and hand strength. A dull or improperly used scraper can cause base damage.

Scrape until there are no obvious low spots—these will appear as a different color or structure. The scraper will not reach down into the "valleys." Carry on scraping until the base is a uniform color and/or structure. You do not need to scrape all the way to the tip, and you should be careful not to scrape down too much at the "break" of the tail, as it is easy to eliminate the groove(s) this way.

To eliminate "waves" in the base, angle the scraper across the ski, rather than scraping at 90° to the length of the ski (refer back to figure 7).

## Sanding

Sanding certainly produces a flat, smooth ski, and it does an excellent job of removing "aged" P-Tex while leaving good structure. In fact, when a base has hardened or fused, sanding can be an excellent way of breaking through the tough outer skin that can form. If your scraper is not sufficiently sharp, or if you are not yet sure of your skills with a scraper, sanding requires less skill and can be a good way to flatten and smooth the base of your skis. Sanding does, however, take a good deal of time, and it can leave hair on the base, which must be removed (by either scraping or buffing, as described below).

You will need a supply of wet-and-dry sandpaper from 80 grit on up to 220 or 320 (a sheet of 400 can be used as a final polish). Use the best you can find: "conventional" sandpaper sheds "sand" into the base and can't be cleaned, while wet-and-dry paper holds up very well and can be cleaned in water. Further, there are very "high-tech" sandpapers which tightly control the size and orientation of the grit, and these are worth looking for. Some have a plastic film, rather than paper, and these are preferable.

Other tools include:
- a form bench
- a firm sanding block (I prefer a wood block; a rubber block will bend, resulting in rounded edges)
- a bucket of water, possibly slightly soapy
- a buffing pad and a block to back it with, or a roto tool that will hold a rotary buffing pad
- a bronze brush
- a sharp steel scraper

Douse the ski with water, and keep the base of the ski wet all through the sanding operation. This helps to wash away the base material as it is sanded off, and keeps the paper from loading up as quickly; it may also contribute to keeping the base cool at the point of contact.

Sand in one direction only, from tip to tail. Research by Toko indicated that skis worked in one direction were faster than those worked in two directions; "unidirectional" work aligned the base material in a uniform fashion and seemed to affect speed positively. One-way work is not a bad habit to develop: if for no other reason, working a ski the same way each time will allow you to reproduce your work more accurately.

If you use a rubber sanding block, a good trick is to sand with the rounded side of the sanding block down. As you pass the block down the length of the ski, gradually rotate it so that new grit is presented to the base all the time. This will keep the paper from loading up as fast, and as new "teeth" are constantly presented the paper will be able to cut more effectively. This may also result in something closer to the interrupted, or random, structure produced by stone-grinding. However, this method will not eliminate "waves" in the base, as the rounded back will simply follow the rise and fall of the surface of the base.

Clean the paper in the water frequently to remove wax and/or P-Tex buildup. It may help to keep a brush or file card on hand for this.

Assuming that the base needs more than just a "once-over" (in which case, you are better off with a steel scraper), start sanding with a coarse paper, 80 or 100 grit. Sand until there are no obvious low spots—these will appear as a different color or structure because the sandpaper will not reach down into the "valleys." Carry on sanding until the base is a uniform color and/or structure. As with scraping, it is not necessary to sand all the way to the tip, and you should be careful not to sand down too much at the "break" of the tail, as it is easy to eliminate the groove(s) this way.

From this point, there are two courses to take: sanding to a polish, or sanding to a given grit in order to leave structure.

**To sand to a polish** (and add structure later), continue to sand the ski, moving through progressively finer grades of sandpaper. You can make this easier by giving the base a light steel scraping with a sharp steel scraper between sandings, as this will shave off some of the hair raised by the sanding process.

When you have reached the last and finest grit, which may

take half an hour per ski, finish the base by removing all the hair, then apply structure (see Chapter 9).

**To structure the ski with sandpaper,** sand only to the grit that will give you a very good "random structure" to meet the conditions at hand. Recommended grits for this purpose are:

Wet snow—100–150 grit
Medium snow—150–220 grit
Cold snow—220–320 grit

If you choose to stop at a given grit for final texturing, it is still *essential to remove all hair,* using one of the following methods.

### Removing Hair

One method is to steel-scrape, making light passes with a very sharp scraper; alternate with bronze-brushing. Or you can buff vigorously with a buffing pad; initially it may work best to buff in two directions. Here again, alternate buffing with bronze-brushing (see the following section).

Either of these processes may be helped by finish-sanding with a very fine paper, say 400–600 grit. This will not alter structure very much, and it will reduce the amount of hair somewhat.

To finish, iron on a very hard wax. This will "float" whatever hair is left. When the wax is fully cooled, scrape with a sharp steel or plastic scraper to "pop" the hair off.

As soon as you are done, "resoak" the base with a soft wax.

### Buffing Pads and Brushes

All the various buffing pads sold by different wax companies will do a good job on your skis.

Most pads consist of an abrasive "sand" embedded in a plastic fiber. Thus, these pads can be thought of as fine, shredded sandpaper, and microscopic inspection shows that while they do remove visible hair, they can create very fine, microscopic hair. For this reason, it is important to do your final buffing with the finest pad you can find, and then apply a layer of hard wax to "pop" what hair is left.

The 3M Heavy Duty Stripping Pad, found in most paint departments, appears at first sight to be awfully aggressive, but the relatively coarse quality of the fibers makes the pad slower to load up, and it does a very good, fast job.

It is best to use a buffing pad with a block; a bronze brush makes a very good block for these pads.

Use buffing pads with a good deal of pressure, always work tip to tail, and make ten or twenty passes with it. The pad can be cleaned with hot water and some soap after it loads up, but when it begins to feel dull, start a new one.

If you have roto tools, use them. This will produce the desired effect much faster than will doing the job by hand. Be aware that it is possible to burn a base by using a roto tool at too high a speed, or lingering too long in one spot.

## Stone-Grinding

Stone-grinding is the most complex way of preparing the base of a ski. It is probably also the best way, and skiers usually report that their skis really take off after grinding.

Stone-grinding accomplishes a number of things: it flattens the base; it removes a layer of P-Tex, exposing new base that will accept wax better; and it is an effective way to provide excellent, long-lasting structure (we will look at structuring in Chapter 9). Skis that have been stone-ground, by a qualified service, will often outglide hand-prepared skis over a wide variety of conditions.

*It is important to realize that poor stone-grinding can cause a great deal of damage to ski bases.* The worst damage is by overheating the base, and thus "fusing" it so that it will not accept wax. Too much grinding can also damage the base. Although a good job can result in an almost "hairless" base, poor grinding can produce "hair." If so, after the ski has been ground you will probably have to work the base thoroughly with a Fibertex or similar pad. A roto tool which will hold a buffing pad is very useful at this stage.

The success of grinding, then, depends on having a very experienced operator with good equipment. If you are not sure that you have a highly qualified operator for the grinder, it is better not to have your skis ground. And remember: you can do almost as good a job by hand as any but the very best operators—who are few and far between. But if you can find a really good stone-grinding service, that is the way to go. It is a fast process for someone with the skill, experience, and equipment.

After a ski has been ground, avoid using a steel scraper on it, and try to be gentle with the structure in order to make it last longer. However, as the structure has been cut in, as opposed to pressed in (see the next chapter), stone-ground structure lasts a long time.

Any thorough reworking of the base will "dry out" the base, and indications are that "aging" of the base begins immediately. Therefore, after grinding and scraping, the skis should be waxed as thoroughly as possible (see Chapter 10) before being used.

A flat, "open" base lays the foundation for good glide and good wax adhesion. The next step in preparing the ski is to structure the base, which we will discuss in the next chapter.

**Chapter**

# STRUCTURE

Structuring the base of your skis is the last stage before applying wax. By putting small grooves—**rills**—in the base of the ski, you can relieve the suction caused by the water film between the ski and the snow. If a greater amount of water is present, more structure is needed. Conversely, the less water present, the less, or finer, the structure can be.

## Structuring Methods

There are two ways of putting structure into a base: by pressing, or by cutting.

**Pressed structure** is pressed into the base with a tool called a **riller**. This type of structure does not need much "de-hairing," if any at all, nor is it as permanent as cut structure: pressed structure will eventually come out of the base, through use. The advantage is that pressed structure is easier to change as conditions change, or if you wish to experiment.

**Cut structures** are more permanent and, if they are applied by a stone grinder, much more precise than any kind of pressed structure. There used to be a few rillers on the market that cut structure into the base; avoid these. As suggested in the previous chapter, only entrust a stone-grinding job to a skilled operator.

An unstable ski can be stabilized to a surprising extent by broad rilling. If you have a pair of unstable skis, try rilling them with a 3-millimeter riller. This looks very "mean," but it works!

Some structure is always needed. But *almost* the right structure is generally as good as *exactly* the right structure, and it takes rigorous testing to tell the difference. Keep it simple, and get out there and ski!

## Patterns of Structure

### Linear Structures

Linear structures, with long, parallel rills, are usually best suited to drier, finer snows. They can be applied by stone-grinding, but are easily applied "in the field" with some kind of rilling tool. A riller with several interchangeable "blades" is the one I use the most, and rillers with rolling "blades" can be good. Bar rillers can also be used, and are cheaper and simpler. The longer bars are easier to hold and control.

### Cross Structures

Cross structures, where the rill pattern crosses the ski and spills water off to one side or the other, are for use in wetter snow. Cross structures can be done with some stone grinders, or by angling a riller bar or wire brush across the ski.

### Random Structure

Random structure is any structure where the "grooves" stop and start. This kind of pattern has usually been the most successful structure across a very broad range of conditions, probably due to the fact that a random, or interrupted, structure spills suction, while a linear structure only carries it along down the base of the ski. Also, it may be that many tiny rills spill more suction than do a few large ones, actually providing more rills per inch.

A rolling riller with a special interrupted pattern will press a broken structure into the base, which should work like random structure. I have not tested these, but they look like a very good idea.

There are quite a few ways to apply random structure:

**Stone-grinding** produces, almost necessarily, some kind of random structuring. Properly managed, stone-grinding will provide all the structure needed.

**Sanding** produces random structure, depending on the grit of the sandpaper used, but sanding requires a great deal of care to eliminate all hair, and should never be used unless there is plenty of time for mopping up operations.

**Rilling** with two different sizes of rilling bars, one over the other, has been very successful in medium and very humid conditions. Use a coarse riller first, then go over the base again with a finer blade. Using a 1-millimeter riller combined with a .75-millimeter has been very successful, as has a .75-millimeter with a .5-millimeter. "Mismatching" the blades causes the rills to spill over into each other, and the result is either cross-rilling or random rilling, depending on how you look at it.

Rilling produces little or no hair, and is well suited for last-minute structuring—but do it before waxing!

**Structuring with a steel brush** is also very effective at producing a random structure. Because it provides many small rills (what we might call "micro-rills"), steel-brush structure can perform effectively up into extremely wet conditions. I have used the steel brush a great deal, and well down into cold, dry snow. The amount of structure produced is a product of how new (and hence sharp) the brush is, the amount of pressure used, and the number of passes.

Note that steel-brushing, especially with a fresh, sharp brush, causes a great deal of hair.

**Combinations**—for example, a 3-millimeter rill first, then a steel brushing—can also be tested, but I have had less success with these. The variations are infinite, however, so the best advice is "Just do it."

**Steel-scraping** also introduces structure, albeit a very fine one (and one that I have yet to find as effective as something a little coarser).

## Structuring Tools and Techniques

To apply structure you will need the following tools:
- a form bench
- a buffing pad
- a bronze brush
- a steel scraper
- a structuring tool

Decide which kind of structuring tool you wish to use, then follow the guidelines below on how to use the various tools available.

**"Box" rillers** are very easy to use, and usually come with several different sizes of rilling "blades." These tools are designed so that they "steer" the tool properly down the length of the ski, and their design holds the rilling "blade" at just the right angle for pressing the rills into the base. It is awkward to change blades often, however, so many technicians prefer the rilling bar. I carry two rillers, each loaded with a different rilling bar already in place, for combination structures. Be careful that the "guides" on the riller do not hit the jaws of your ski vise, causing an interruption in the pattern.

**The rilling bar** is very simple, and looks rather like a file with teeth only on the edges. Use a long one: it is simply a better tool than a short one because it is easy to use both hands, one on each side of the ski, and exert a lot of pressure on the base, thus making very deep rills.

When using the bar, guide it with your thumbs on either side of the ski, in such a way as to ensure straight lines. I prefer to push the bar, others prefer to pull it. It probably doesn't make a great deal of difference which you do, so long as you are in control of the tool, and control is a matter of habit and practice. Use the bar at an angle of around 45° to the base; in this way, the rill is effectively pressed into the base.

**The steel brush**, fondly referred to as the "barbecue brush," looks lethal but can be very useful. Use the brush at a slight angle to the base, as this prevents "chatter." Use a lot of pressure, and five to ten strokes. I prefer to use short strokes, working down the length of the base. It takes experimentation, but this is a versatile and useful tool.

Unfortunately, the life of a steel brush is limited: after a time, the wires lose their edges. You can make up for a dull brush by increasing pressure and/or using more passes, but it is a good idea to replace the brush each season, saving the old one for less aggressive structure, or for juniors.

by removing hair with a bronze brush and a buffing pad or, even better, with a roto tool. Be especially thorough when finishing up after the steel brush, as a fresh brush can make a good deal of hair. It is a good idea to follow the pad with an application of very hard glide wax which you then remove with a sharp steel scraper, to "pop" off whatever hair is still left on the base.

Don't forget to wax the ski thoroughly after structuring!

Now let's move on to wax application.

# APPLYING WAX

The ski has now been flattened, the pores have been opened up so that the base will accept wax, and the base has been structured for the prevailing conditions. Now it is time to apply the glide wax. (Kick-waxing is covered in Chapter 12.)

There are three very important guidelines to follow before applying the wax of the day:

**Read the thermometer!** Wax for snow temperature, unless the temperature is above 0°C, when you will have to wax by air temperature (if the snow is above 0° it ceases to be snow). Snow temperature may well be several hours behind air temperature when the weather is warming. Be sure to listen to weather predictions.

**Read the directions on the wax box!** The goal of the wax companies is to see that you are on the best possible wax, and they have all done considerable research to make sure you are. Be very cautious about second-guessing them!

**Don't be influenced by what anyone else is doing!** You have done your testing, you have checked your thermometers, you have read the label. Trust yourself, and stick to your guns! The other waxer probably doesn't know any more than you do, and he may even be quite wrong. Too many races have been ruined by psychological damage due to listening to too many other wax opinions.

**Stay calm: your wax will usually work well even if conditions change a little.** *Almost* the right glide wax is as good as the right wax.

## Waxing Tools and Techniques

You will need three tools for applying wax:

- a form bench
- a waxing iron
- a respirator

Invest some money in your waxing iron—it will work better, and it will protect your skis. A good iron holds an even heat, and is usually heavy; it should have no steam holes. Travel irons are a delight to pack, but they don't hold much heat, and their temperature fluctuates wildly. Fluctuations do two bad things: if the iron is too cool, it takes forever to melt-in the wax (and a really cold wax may not go in at all); and if the iron is too hot, it can damage the base. Most wax companies market good waxing irons.

Under some circumstances, waxing can be bad for you. Invest in a good mask. This is very important with fluoros, but potentially important with paraffins as well, especially if you are in a room where someone is smoking the wax (making it smoke), which you will be: overly ambitious ironers are with us always. (More on waxing safety in Chapter 14.)

When ironing, *always keep the iron moving*. This prevents too much heat from building up in one place and damaging the base. You can iron one section several times, as when you wax the front and then the back section of your classic skis, or you can run the iron down the entire length of the ski several times. But keep it moving!

*NEVER wax too hot*. This alters the wax and can destroy a base. Even fluorocarbons do not need extremely hot irons (I prefer to cork them, anyway—see Chapter 13), and as for the hard greens, it is better to spend some time rather than vaporize your skis.

Always begin application of your racing wax by "clean-waxing"— that is, the skis should be waxed and scraped at least once before applying a new race wax in order to clean the base. Iron the wax on, scrape thoroughly with a plastic scraper, then brush with a nylon brush. A travel wax that has been applied at home after cleaning the skis will serve the same function.

Begin applying the actual race wax by crayoning a layer of wax directly onto the base. This is a good idea whether you are doing travel wax, "clean wax," or race wax: crayoning provides a thin cover for the base, insulating it from direct contact with the iron and thus protecting it from overheating. In the case of harder waxes, this is a little more difficult than with softer paraffins; it can be done by touching the wax to the iron, then dabbing it onto the base.

Having crayoned-on a layer of wax, you may wish to drip a little more onto the base. It is important to have enough wax to cover the base evenly, and to penetrate, but there's no need to resort to the "dip method." A good crayoning will often suffice, and will make your more expensive waxes go a lot farther.

One good trick, especially with expensive waxes, is to scrape the groove after the iron has passed over the ski a few times; this will pop the wax in the groove back onto the base, where it can be ironed-in for better coverage.

## Mixing Waxes

I very seldom mix waxes. The waxes we use today have broad ranges and good overlap, and the complicated old witches' brews of three oranges with one blue and a dab of red just aren't needed, if they ever were.

If you are mixing waxes, you can do so with a reservoir iron, but these tend to waste a lot of wax. They can be good for teams, but frankly, I never use one; they're too awkward.

There are two other ways to mix the waxes: on the iron, by holding the bars of wax together; or by dripping first one wax on the base, and then the other. If you hold the wax on the iron, the softer wax will melt faster, so be sure to hold the waxes evenly (at 90° to the iron); sandwiching two harder waxes around a softer one will help to ensure a more even mix. If you drip two waxes, as, for example, when the bars are too large to fit the iron, simply try to move each one along the base at equal speeds; 2:1 mixes can be done this way.

A precise mix of waxes is not very important anyway, so don't worry about it too much. It is virtually impossible to tell the difference between a 2.1:1 mixture and a 1.9:1 mixture without a great deal of very precise testing.

In the case of some mixes, it can save time to crayon-on the first layer, say a graphite, then drip-on the second.

I prefer never to mix brands. Ingredients in one brand may cancel out important ingredients in other brands, some ingredients may not mix at all, and separation can occur. Keep it simple!

## Layering

There are many cases where you may wish to have a layer of one wax in the ski, and then add another on top. This is done with some graphite waxes; subsequent waxes will often perform better and/or last longer over a layer of graphite, molybdenum, etc. Or you may subsequently apply a fluorocarbon (see below).

Scrape the sublayer with a sharp plastic scraper, then brush with a nylon or horsehair brush. You should only be interested in what is down in the pores. Scraping and brushing will not affect this; brushing insufficiently, on the other hand, may change the final "mix" adversely.

Racers often apply three layers of wax: a clean wax, then a sublayer, then the fastest paraffin. On fluorocarbon days, I do all this below the fluoro: an antistatic layer for wax and base "endurance," a fluoroparaffin layer for the fluoro to bond to, then the pure fluoro powder or block.

There can also be "superlayering" where an additive needs to be added over or into the main wax. "Hardening waxes," which increase durability and adapt the cold waxes to even colder snows, are added into the main wax while it is being ironed and is warm. Some companies add a graphite wax over the main wax.

## Ironing

I follow this procedure when ironing:
1. Crayon and/or drip the wax on the base.
2. Iron the full length of the ski five or six times.
3. Take the ski off the bench and place it *base up* somewhere where it can continue to absorb the now molten wax.
4. Begin ironing the next ski; when I have waxed ski number two five or six times, it goes onto the rack, and ski number one is waxed again.

5. Continue to alternate several times, with no scraping between ironings, though it may be necessary to add wax, if the base goes "dry."

**Ironing Rule Number One, Two, and Three: If the iron smokes, it is too hot.** (A properly adjusted iron may just smoke when not in active service: without the base to dissipate its heat, it may overheat slightly.)

**Be sure to keep the iron moving.** This helps to keep any one part of the base from overheating, helps to prevent structural damage from too much heat buildup in the core, and ensures an even distribution of wax. Note that tip and tail areas, being thinner, can absorb less heat; be especially careful in these areas.

**Generally, the longer you iron, the greater the wax penetration.** Studies have shown significant wax absorption up to around 13 minutes, or even more. Generally, iron until the wax is liquid along the entire length of the ski, though this rule does not apply to fluorocarbons and the harder waxes such as the greens.

After ironing, I try to remember to scrape the groove. It's easier to do it before the wax cools, especially when using harder glide waxes.

## Some Waxing Tips

Remember that five or more waxings are not too much for a new ski; some keep new skis in a sauna, to keep the wax running.

At the 1997 World Championships in Trondheim, Norway, Bjørn Dæhlie tested a new pair of skis the afternoon before one of the races. After skiing them around for a few minutes, he felt that they were an outstanding pair for the conditions, and decided to race on them the next day. The service staff stone ground the skis, waxed them about twenty times—and Dæhlie won a gold medal on them the next day. Lesson Number One: New skis can be fast! Lesson Number Two: You can't overwax!

Occasionally, wax the sidewalls to protect them and seal the skis from water. The sidewalls are in touch with the snow while skating or cornering, so why not wax them? This can be done with hot wax, or with paste wax.

In some conditions, snow may build up on the top of the ski, throwing it out of balance, perhaps, or making it heavier. To avoid this, you can apply paste wax, or perhaps a layer of car wax, to the top of the ski. Aside from avoiding snow buildup, this will keep the ski looking new, and equipment you can take pride in will deliver a psychological boost (although there is always the opposite approach of winning with the grubbiest skis around— but you have to be very good to pull this one off).

Sludgy spots where the iron refuses to move evenly along the base may indicate a need to add wax (and in any case, do not continue to iron a sludgy spot), or it may indicate a damaged or uneven base. In the former case, add wax; in the latter, scraping or sanding may be indicated.

Always rewax after skiing! After the race or training session— as soon as possible—remove the old wax and/or clean the ski. This will take out accumulated dirt and reopen structure and pores. Clean the ski by brushing it thoroughly with a bronze brush, then apply clean wax or travel wax. This process will pull out remaining dirt when the skis are scraped.

## Wax Removal

If the ski has acquired a layer of grunge, as will happen in dirty snow or when klister is being used, clean it with a wax remover. Apply the remover to a paper towel and wipe it on in sufficient quantity to do the job. If removers are allowed to sit for a minute or two, they work better. Wipe off with a clean towel, dry with another towel, and allow the inevitable remaining remover to evaporate for as long as possible, then apply clean wax.

I try to use removers as sparingly as possible. Wax removers are hard on plastics: Jim Galanes spilled some on the face of a hygrometer once, without noticing. A few minutes later the face was so "curdled" that it was impossible to read the dial.

After using wax remover, always apply a layer of wax, as the remover dries out the base. *Never* apply remover to a hot or warm base, as this accelerates the drying out and can affect the base adversely.

I prefer the new citron-based removers, as they are supposed to be less toxic (or even nontoxic), and I believe they work better, anyway.

## Travel-Waxing

Please, *never* travel without waxing your skis! A layer of wax on the base

- protects the ski from dirt
- protects the skis from rubbing against each other, thus preventing scratches
- has them ready to go next time (try to anticipate the conditions where you will use the ski next, and travel-wax accordingly)

In a real emergency, you can travel-wax by crayoning a layer of wax onto the base before traveling. Some iron-in a layer, then drip a few dots onto the base, adding still better separation. And as long as we're on the subject, please do two more things to protect your skis:

- Always travel with skis in a ski bag to protect them from dirt.
- Tie them together with something that separates the bases; never just clamp or tie them together, which has been the cause of untold scratch damage. Most companies make "ski ties" just for this, and there are also "dog bones" which hold and separate the skis. If you can't find this kind of holder, slip old socks over the tip and tail before you tie the skis together.

Now the skis are almost ready to put on the snow, and only final preparation—scraping and brushing—remains, if you are preparing classic skis, to be followed by kick-waxing.

# FINAL PREPPING

The skis are now almost ready: flattened, structured, and waxed for the snow conditions of the race or training day.

It's always a good idea to wax the afternoon or night before. This way all the heavy work is done, and you can concentrate on a good night's sleep; and in the morning you can focus on a good warm-up and the race.

If any changes are in order, due to different weather than was expected, it is very easy to rewax quickly when all the cleaning and sublayering has been done already. One morning at the World Championships in Falun, Sweden, in 1993, we had a significant weather change, but because skis had been made ready the day before, we were able to run an early-morning glide test, then rewax about ten pairs of skis in 45 minutes.

If any last-minute wax changes are called for, simply brush thoroughly, calmly rewax, and allow the ski sufficient cool-down time to get to room temperature.

Avoid last-minute wax panic! If changes are only marginal, you may well be better off to leave the ski alone ("If it works, don't fix it") and concentrate on a good warm-up. Being flexible, skied-in, warmed-up, and calm are all far more important than minor wax adjustments. Of course, in the case of kick wax, you can go on refining right up to start time.

Before you scrape your skis, give them ample time to cool, and let them cool slowly. Different brands of skis cool at different speeds, depending on the core material, so it's a good idea to allow as much time as you can for cooling down to room temperature. This is because rapid cooling, such as setting the ski outside, encourages the wax to "crack" off the ski, while scraping a ski too warm can take some of the structure out of the base.

For final prepping, you will need:

- a form bench
- a plastic scraper (sharp)
- a plastic scraper sharpener, or a block and a file or some sandpaper
- brushes

## Scraping

Always scrape with a plastic scraper when removing wax for final prepping. This is not the time to remove base material, or to structure. Always scrape on a form bench.

Make sure your plastic scraper is sharp. Plastic scrapers can and should be sharpened often: use a ceramic scraper sharpener, or a file, or even sandpaper. If you use either of the latter two, hold the scraper against a block of wood, to ensure a good 90° angle on the scraper, much the same way we made sure of a 90° edge on the steel scraper (figure 8).

Really hard waxes need to be scraped warm. If you scrape these waxes cold, they simply "pop" off the base and out of the pores, and wax coverage will be poor. Scraping them cold also causes a shower of splinters, and these can get in your eyes.

*Figure 8. Sharpening a plastic scraper on a piece of sandpaper. Note the use of the wood block, to ensure a 90-degree edge. Be sure to put the sandpaper on a flat surface!*

Some experts scrape these waxes as soon as they finish ironing. At the Start factory, I was told to iron one end of the ski with Start green and Arctic, scrape it, then iron the other end and scrape.

If you scrape warm, however, try not to scrape with a great deal of pressure; warm bases are plastic, in the strict sense of the word, and you can alter structure by "massaging" it out of the ski if you scrape a hot ski aggressively.

Don't forget the groove! In fact, it is a good idea to scrape the groove as soon as you are done ironing, as this will make life simpler later on, when you scrape after cooling. Use a klister spreader/ groove scraper or, in the case of very small grooves, perhaps the corner of a plastic scraper. But remember that clearing the groove helps the stability of the ski, as well as its speed, and eliminates exposed wax that can pick up dirt.

## Brushing

After scraping, brush thoroughly to reopen structure and remove any excess wax. Many people use a nylon brush or a combi brush for this. A horsehair brush will do an excellent job putting on a final polish, and I've been told that horsehair raises less static electricity than nylon.

Brush thoroughly. Remember, you are both removing excess wax, and "polishing" out a thin film of wax on the surface of the base. Roto brushes are easier and faster, and a real time saver with multiple pairs—but you can do just as good a job by hand!

After scraping very cold and hard waxes, some technicians polish with a nylon stocking stretched over a cork, or with some Fiberlene or a piece of cloth. I feel that thorough brushing, especially with a roto brush, does a very good job of polishing.

Once you have brushed, wipe off the ski with a towel, some Fiberlene, even a sleeve, in order to get the last stray bits of wax off the base.

Put the skis outside to cool. It is a good idea not to ski until the ski has reached snow temperature, otherwise the heat in the ski will cause melting (which can lead to icing), and the wax, being softer, will be more liable to wear.

In very cold weather, allow the ski to cool outside, then bring it back in for another brushing and a final polish with the nylon or a bit of cloth. This is done because as the ski cools, it contracts and extrudes paraffin; rebrushing will remove excess paraffin and smooth the wax film. Also, a ski that is set out in cold weather will often ice a little, owing to condensation. Rebrushing will rid the base of ice.

### Some Pointers on Roto Brushes

- Rotate the brush in such a way that the bristles pass over the base in a tip-to-tail direction.
- The increased efficiency of the roto brush has made bronze-brushing less common; for cleaning skis, use a combi brush, with mixed natural and fiber bristles.
- For a finer finish, use a dedicated horsehair brush for paraffins, and another for fluorocarbons. Mark each brush prominently!

It takes a lot of power to turn a brush, so either use a plug-in hand drill, or be sure to get the most powerful battery-driven drill you can find, with a fast charger and at least one spare battery. I prefer to roto brush at high speed: the centrifugal force has the effect of "stiffening" the bristles in the brush.

### Pre-start Brushing

Often a final brushing just before the start will speed a ski up again. Whether this is due to smoothing out cold-extruded paraffin, or to removing accumulations of dirt, I don't know—but it works. As the wax is now pretty hard, a combi brush may be a good idea, though nylon or horsehair will also work. For fluoros, use a horsehair fluoro brush, and this last brushing will add just a bit more fluoro to the base.

If you can, do this on a form bench. It's a good idea to have one set up near the starting line; anyway, on classic days, it is very valuable to have a bench handy for last-minute tune-ups.

Now the skis are ready to go, unless you are preparing classic skis. If that is the case, it's now time to turn our attention to kick-waxing.

# 12
**Chapter**

# KICK-WAXING

Kick-waxing is special. Unlike the relative simplicity of glide-waxing, where pretty good is really about good enough, when it comes to kick, if you're out of it, you aren't going to get back into it.

On a classic technique day, kick is *everything*. And even if the kick isn't all that bad, poor kick-waxing can result in poor technique. It's all very well to say you have to "tough" it out, but to ski well you have to have reasonable to very good kick.

Let's go back for a moment to review why wax provides kick. Snow crystals dig into the wax layer, providing traction, in much the same way that sand digs into the rubber of a tire, and with the same effect: traction. But here the analogy ends, and for two reasons: (1) a rough wax surface does not provide good grip; and (2) a smooth wax surface is necessary to good glide.

We used to think that globbing wax onto a ski would provide traction, much the same way that the knobs on a snow tire provide traction for your car. On the contrary, a rough wax layer prevents the snow from pressing into the wax surface equally in all areas, resulting in less grip, while at the same time producing friction. Chain your tires, not your skis!

It's a mistake to look at kick-waxing as something arcane and difficult. Kick-waxing is part of the art and science of cross-country skiing. There are few things to equal the satisfaction and delight of a really good kick-wax job. In the following pages, we'll have a look at a number of techniques and ideas, but in the end it all comes back to the same rules that held for glide-waxing:

Read the snow and air thermometers!

Read the directions on the wax box!
Don't be influenced by what anyone else is doing!
And above all, keep it simple!

## Choice of Kick Wax

**Read the label!** There are many kick waxes on the market; almost all of them are very good. But it still takes time to learn to use specific waxes—when they will work, how much to use, how they last—so don't forget to find out what conditions the manufacturer designed the wax for.

The best way to become an effective waxer is to stick to one brand, and really learn how to use it. This cannot be overemphasized. Especially with juniors, keep it as simple as possible. Carrying several different brands of wax around simply leads to confusion and not really knowing how to use them. I carry one main brand of kick wax in my box, with just a few other old favorites from other brands.

**Read the thermometer!** Carry two thermometers. You are waxing for the snow, not the air, but air warmer than the snow is an indicator that the snow temperature will likely rise.

Take snow temperature close to the surface—that's what you're skiing on. Deeper readings will often be colder, and can indicate that the snow may remain cold in spite of warmer air.

Once you have read thermometers and labels, the real test is how the wax actually works (testing is discussed in depth in Part 3). Remember that a wax may well take some skiing-in: at the World Championships in Thunder Bay, Ontario, in 1995, Michel De Sutter tried on his race skis, and told us they were slipping. We told him to ski them in, and when he came back after a kilometer or two, he said they were perfect. In fact, he later told me that they were the best race skis he had ever had. The moral: Be patient.

## Kick-Waxing Tools and Techniques

You will need the following tools for applying wax:
- a form bench, if at all possible
- corks or klister spreaders
- a blowtorch or hot-air gun

Apply kick wax in thin layers. Multiple thin layers are better than one or two thick layers: they are much easier to smooth, and a smooth wax job both kicks and glides better.

Heating the first layer of wax onto the base will usually make it last longer. Allow the wax to cool, smooth it out with a cork, then apply subsequent layers. Do not cork warm wax! Follow this sequence:

1. Crayon the wax onto the base.
2. Iron (optional).
3. Cool.
4. Cork again.
5. Apply subsequent layers.

Clean your iron after heating-in a kick wax or a binder to avoid getting grip wax/binder into your glide wax next time you use the iron.

There is no difference in speed between ironed-in or corked-in layers. I prefer always to heat-in the first layer. Speed comes from the right wax, and from good corking. Subsequent layers need not be ironed-in: the purpose of the ironing is to get the wax into the pores of the base.

## Corks and Corking

Given a good pair of skis and a wax somewhere reasonably close to the right hardness, probably the most frequent cause of both poor kick and poor glide is careless or improper corking. I learned this at the World Championships in Val di Fiemme, Italy, in 1991. Jim Galanes and I were out testing wax, and we exchanged skis—same glide wax, same kick wax. Jim's skis felt as fast as skating skis, but with kick. The reason: Jim's corking skills.

The cork is the most important tool in your wax box, along with your scraper, and using it is as much an art. A skier who wishes to master the art of skiing cannot afford to neglect something so basic as the proper use of the cork. *Ars longa, vita brevis est.* Corking takes practice.

Foam corks work better; avoid "cork corks." Foam corks create friction-generated heat sooner, which is what makes the wax smooth out, and they tend to hold together better.

It can be a good idea to dedicate corks to certain uses: a really well equipped wax box will have a cork for low- and high-temperature waxes, possibly one (or more) for graphite waxes and tars, another for binders, and still another for klister-hard wax mixes.

Sound like a lot of corks? It may not be worth it, but at least have kick wax corks, and a binder cork! Mark the corks according to their intended use, using a felt marker pen (add your initials, and be very unfriendly to people who borrow your corks).

Waxes will go on more evenly if applied cool, and if applied in many thin layers. Except for the first layer, I prefer to do all corking outdoors, where it is cold. Corking indoors will often allow the wax to become too warm, and when this happens, it will begin to drag and get lumpy or to streak or glob while you cork. Corking is best done on a form bench; I try to set one up wherever I'm race-waxing, and as close as possible to the track, so that testing and adjustments can be done with a minimum of running back and forth and general fuss.

Generally, use light, fast motions, with the cork flat against the wax. A cork works by creating heat through friction, but too much pressure or heat can drag the wax around, and will begin to create globs and holes. If this begins to happen, stop, and allow the wax to cool before starting again. When you start again, be sure to use light, quick motions. This method is a must for corking binders.

Use high-pressure passes with the cork to spread wax, especially with a first and/or thick layer. However, more than a few passes this way can result in lumping or pulling the wax around too much. Use the edge of the cork to smooth out globs, in long, fairly high-pressure movements.

Finish by using the corner or edge of the cork down the groove, perhaps followed by another pass or two down the whole kick wax area.

To "proof" your corking, look for the following:

- The wax should be virtually invisible and transparent when you are done corking, and there should be no white spots, which indicate either air or water in the wax.
- There should be no globs or holes in the wax surface.

All this takes practice, errors, and experience—and the errors are as important as the successes in the learning process. But good corking can make a very substantial difference in ski performance, as well as in technique and results. Experiment and learn!

## Binders

Many skiers feel that roughing up the base of the ski in the kick area helps wax adhesion. This will certainly help if the pores have been closed by use of too much heat when removing wax. Use a sandpaper of around 120–180 grit, and rub the base fairly gently; the idea is to open the base, but not to create a lot of "hair," which can have a slowing effect.

A difficult choice is whether or not to use a binder to hold your kick wax on. If you are in abrasive conditions where heavy wax wear is expected (snow that has been heavily groomed, artificial snow, icy patches, or a long race), a binder may be in order.

Choice of ski is important when the snow may indicate use of a binder: a stiffer ski may not need binder as much, while a too-soft ski may shed wax so fast as to make binder useless. Courses can also affect the decision to use binder or not: a lot of hard downhill corners may accelerate wax wear; stepping corners is easier on wax than side-slipping.

The problem is that if you wear down to the binder, the skis may become very slow and lose kick. In new snow, binder can be deadly to glide. As a rule, only use binder if necessary, use it sparingly, and get it smooth.

There are two common ways to apply binder. The first is to crayon it onto the base. This method will often work best if the binder is cool, and it will work only if the base is dry. Then heat the binder with a blowtorch, hot-air gun, or iron. I prefer an iron, as the iron will smooth the binder as it heats it in (a blowtorch can burn the base).

The second technique is to "rag" the binder in: using a torch or air gun and a piece of Fiberlene as a "brush," spread and smooth the binder, while at the same time heating it thoroughly.

Let the binder cool, then smooth it out with a cork before applying kick wax. It is a good idea to dedicate a cork to binder, to avoid mixing binder in with the kick wax. Cork with light pressure, preferably on a form bench; swift passes are best.

When applying kick wax over binder, I prefer to alternate skis between each layer. Alternating skis will help to avoid heating the wax, which would allow it to mix with the binder, and/or lump up. You can also *cautiously* iron or torch the wax; this will improve the wax to binder adhesion. Allow to cool again. Apply several more layers of kick wax.

Three ironclad rules apply when using binder:

- Heat the binder in well.
- Make sure the binder is *thin* and smooth. Often a mere "tacky" layer will be enough. Too much can be very slow.
- Allow the binder to cool thoroughly. Place the ski outdoors, and let it cool to outside temperature before adding kick wax. If the binder is not cool, you will not be able to apply kick wax properly!

## Layering

You may wish to layer waxes—for example, when mixing in graphite wax or a tar. In this case, you can cork vigorously, as the object is to mix the waxes.

When putting a harder wax over a softer wax to improve glide, you will need to cork more gently, to avoid mixing.

Tars and fluorinated waxes are often best applied over a layer of "normal" wax to act as a "binder."

## Rescue Operations

With an uneven base, or an uneven cork, it may be easier to cork just one side of the ski at a time, holding the cork lengthwise to the ski on one side of the groove, rather than across.

If a hard wax starts to drag and get lumpy, you can:

- Use light, quick motions; this is the most common first-aid method.
- Allow it to cool, then recork.
- Use the edge of the cork, and high pressure, and smooth out the wax as if you were using a putty knife.
- Bring it in and smooth it with an iron, then recork when it cools.

## Zero-Degree Conditions and "Hairies"

In zero-degree conditions, when nothing on earth seems to work, when every known wax either ices or slips, or both, try "hairies." This is a way of making extremely effective no-wax bases which will usually work when nothing else will—and if you hit it right, hairies kick like roller skis.

Rough up the base with an abrader or with 60–80-grit sandpaper: rub the kick zone until the base is, quite literally, hairy. Avoid sideways motion, and keep the abraded area to a length a little inside your normal kick zone. Apply silicone or a fluorocarbon powder to avoid icing.

To remove hairies, use a steel scraper. You can't do this to a base too many times, so either be sure you need hairies, or keep a pair of medium-flex skis dedicated to this use.

Other zero-degree options include the following procedure, familiarly known as a "Wop Job" (no offense intended here): apply a layer of binder, then mix in a layer of 0°C wax such as a yellow, using the ragging method (use a rolled-up piece of Fiberlene like a paintbrush, and alternate passes with the Fiberlene with passes with a blowtorch). Allow the mixture to cool thoroughly, then cover with extra-blue or multigrade, and cork smooth. *Cooling the mixed layer is essential.* It may be necessary to heat the cover wax with a torch to get it to go on over the mixed layer, but do not allow the mixed layer and the cover layer to mix. Cork gently, alternate skis, work outside.

Somewhat similar to this is a *thin* layer of silver klister which is allowed to cool, then covered with violet or multigrade. Try not to mix the klister and the cover.

## Klister

When the snow has metamorphosed—in other words, thawed and refrozen—the crystal becomes large and rounded. In order to get "kick," or traction, the wax has to be soft enough for the larger, rounded crystals to dig into it: hence klister, which remains soft even when cold. You can get incredible kick from klisters, but they have a well-deserved bad reputation owing to their general stickiness and their perverse love of oozing all over everything from your hands to the bottom of the wax box, to the roof of your car. Public Safety Announcement: Put the lid back on the klister tube after using it, and put the tube back in its box.

Most people tend to apply too much klister. Dab it onto the base from the tube; then, using your thumb and a hot-air gun or blowtorch, spread it and smooth it out. The heat will also help to bind the klister to the base.

Do not use a torch to smooth out fluoro klisters! The flame of a torch is hot enough to release dangerous gases from the fluoros. Use an iron!

You can also smooth out klister with the heel of your hand, moving slowly to allow the heat from your hand to soften the klister. However, this will not always result in good adhesion; it is better to heat and smooth it with a torch or hot-air gun.

Try to apply klister near an electricity source, so you can heat it with a hot-air gun; or be sure to bring along a propane torch (butane torches are just a little better than useless), and try to find one of the self-lighting kind.

In the absence of heat, keep the tube under your armpit or inside your clothes; this will keep it warm enough to make spreading it on the ski possible. To smooth, try corking, using fast strokes down the whole length of the kick zone.

If you have heated a klister, never put the ski down on the snow until it is cool, or it will ice.

If you have to add or change klister, do not add new klister over wet and/or dirty klister. Remove as much of the previous application as you can, using a spatula. Putting more klister over wet klister is a prime source of icing and grabbing.

Like kick waxes, klisters are never brushed.

Here are a few guidelines when using klister:

- Avoid klister if at all possible: on a well-groomed track, it is often possible to find a hard wax that will grip just as well, and run faster.
- In abrasive conditions, use a blue or violet klister as a binder, although blues can freeze and chip off.
- Experiment with hard wax binder under klister; it can sometimes resist the chipping that klister binders are prone to in cold conditions. Or try mixing hard wax binder and blue klister.

- Add silver to increase glide and/or prevent icing. This won't always work, but it's worth a try.
- Around 0°C, try silvers or universals.
- Before racing, remove klister from the sidewalls and, using a spatula, remove any that has run past the end of the kick zone.
- Be sure klister is *fully cooled* before skiing on it!
- Put the cap back on the tube!

## Cleaning

To clean your skis, remove as much of the wax or klister as you easily can, using a putty knife. This will be easier if you sharpen the edge of the knife somewhat, but be careful not to make it too sharp, as the knife will then be inclined to cut into the base. After you have removed most of the wax from the base and sidewall, apply wax remover, using the corner of a rag, a piece of Fiberlene, or a paper towel. Allow this to work for a few moments, then remove the wax remover and wax with Fiberlene, rubbing the base as much as needed to get all the wax off. Then take a fresh piece of Fiberlene, and remove the "varnish" that remains.

Try not to get excess wax remover into the glide zones of the ski, as this will both remove glide wax and deposit a film of dissolved kick wax.

After using wax remover, apply a quick layer of wax and scrape it off to remove residue. You can also use this layer as a travel wax; just be sure to wax the ski once to clean it, before applying the actual glide wax you will be using.

Never use wax remover on a warm base, as this accelerates the drying-out of the base material drastically.

Use wax remover sparingly: it is not good for plastics!

## Kick-Waxing Secrets and Junior Racing

I'm of two minds about "secrets" when kick-waxing. On the one hand, the best skier ought to win the race, but on the other, waxing is as much a part of the art of cross-country skiing as are training, technique, and all the rest—so the person who is the better waxer should have the advantage. Still, I hate to see a race decided, on a complicated day, by wax. Here are two things I feel very strongly about, especially in regard to junior racing:

**Juniors should not win races on wax.** Coaches should exchange information on waxes at this level, where it really is the skiing that counts. Somebody having a bad day because of the wax is not good for our sport, or for the athlete's growth and development. For this reason I also feel that fluoros should not be used in junior competition (see the end of the next chapter).

**Young skiers should learn to wax their own skis**—especially the girls, who so often aren't given a chance to do their own waxing. Young skiers must be encouraged to learn these techniques. Learning to wax is part of the sport, and not encouraging kids to learn to wax is to deprive them of knowledge and skills that will be essential to their success and enjoyment later on. Please, coaches: Make your kids wax their own skis! Try making a game of it ("Who can put on four layers of blue the smoothest?").

# Part 3

# SOME FURTHER CONSIDERATIONS

The first two parts of this book covered the basics, and by the end of Chapter 12, the skis should be ready to go. Now it's time to take a look at several areas that fall outside of general, day-to-day use.

# 13
**Chapter**

# FLUOROCARBONS

The uses, application, dangers—and even implications—of fluorocarbon "waxes" are so different from those of normal paraffin-based waxes that the subject deserves a separate chapter of its own.

Mechanically, fluorocarbons form a thin film or membrane on the base of the ski. To this extent, they are much like regular paraffins, only more so—because fluoros are extremely hydrophobic (water-repelling), much more long-lasting than paraffins, and quite dirt resistant.

There are now many fluorocarbons on the market. All are good, and all are superior to paraffins in certain conditions:

**In high humidity**, especially in new-fallen or falling snow, fluoros will be faster than paraffins. Fluoros can be used at surprisingly low temperatures if the humidity remains high. We used fluoros very successfully in Anchorage when the temperature was -15°C, but the humidity was around 80 percent.

**In wet conditions**, fluorocarbons may not be fastest initially. Their advantage will sometimes only kick in *at long distances*, where they will be faster owing to the fact that they are tougher than paraffins, and resist dirt.

**In dirty snow**, fluoros are a genuine advantage because of their ability to resist dirt. Dirt does not adhere to, or become imbedded in, fluoros as easily as it does in paraffins, especially the soft paraffins associated with warm and wet snow conditions.

**In very wide temperature ranges**, if a fluoro is not the "right wax," it will usually not be far wrong. Fluoros are forgiving over a broad range of conditions, which makes them a safe guess when you are in doubt.

In low humidity it is important to remember that waxes with little or no fluoro content may well be faster than a fluoro combination. Partly because they are expensive and "hi tech" there is a trend toward over-use of fluoros.

Fluorocarbons perform better over a sublayer. This can be a graphite wax, a fluoroparaffin, or even the fastest paraffin of the day. These sublayers prepare the base for better adhesion of the final, pure fluoro layer; more on this below. Fluoros can be ironed on or corked in.

## Fluorocarbon "Formats"

There are two "formats" of fluorocarbons on the market: the powders, and the solids. There is no difference between the two; the original fluoros were in powder form, but when the solid form was introduced, it became clear that the block was much more economical to use: no more powder falling off onto the table.

Solid fluoros can also be used as part of a "panic kit," to be crayoned on and corked in at the last moment, should there be a change in conditions. Simply crayon the solids on, then iron or cork, then brush.

If you use the powders, a 30-gram canister of fluoro should do for five or six pairs of skis, so gauge the amount you put on accordingly. Note that using too little fluorocarbon powder can expose the base to undue direct heat.

**Fluoroparaffins.** Fluoroparaffins are waxes that combine fluorocarbons with "normal" paraffins. They consist of a molecular chain with paraffin components at one end, and fluorocarbon components at the other. Because paraffins chemically resemble the material ski bases are made of, paraffins penetrate into the base better than do fluorocarbons. The paraffin end of the molecule thus attaches to the base, while the fluorocarbon components remain on the outside, and are "anchored" there by the deeper-penetrating paraffins.

Fluoroparaffins have become very common, and have proven to be not just a compromise between paraffins and fluoros, but quite effective in themselves. Fluoroparaffins can perform very well on their own, being both faster and better-lasting in some conditions than non-fluorinated paraffins, and are effective as a sublayer for fluorocarbons.

## How to Apply Fluoros

There are two ways to apply fluorocarbons. I will first explain the "traditional" technique, and then we'll look at some new developments.

### The "Traditional" Way

Structure the skis, and apply sublayers. After ironing the sublayer in, scrape and brush the base thoroughly.

In my wax box I keep a used fluoro lid into which I have bored holes, rather like a coarse salt shaker (a salt shaker might be very useful for this). I snap this onto the fluoro container when we are applying fluoros, then simply sprinkle the fluoro onto the base, as evenly as possible.

Sprinkle or rub the fluoro on, then rub it in as evenly as possible with your thumb or with a dedicated cork to assure more even coverage.

Having applied the fluoro, iron it at an appropriate temperature. The iron does not need to be any hotter to apply fluorocarbons than it does to apply a hard paraffin. *Do not iron fluoros too hot,* as this will damage the base of the ski.

Make one slow pass down the length of the ski with the iron—that's all (though you may need to go back and hit spots that are still white). The signs of correct ironing temperature are:

- the "light show": the sparkles that flash around behind the iron (note that some fluoros do not do this)
- the fluoro "disappears": white spots indicate the need for a touch-up

Allow the ski to cool to room temperature, and brush thoroughly with a horsehair brush (see "Brushing," below).

### A New Direction

A number of new techniques for application of fluorocarbons have emerged over the last season or two, which seem to result in markedly increased ski speeds. A little background on these developments should help make the process clearer.

There is evidence that fluorocarbons are more prone to static electric buildup than are paraffins. Therefore, it is important to sublayer fluorocarbons with a compound that contains electrically conductive material such as graphite, iron oxide, molybdenum, etc., as these materials will help to disperse static charges.

Fluorocarbons bond best to fluorocarbons. This indicates that sublayering fluoros with a fluoroparaffin should result in better adhesion. Testing has indicated that fluorinated paraffins make better sublayers.

Ironing fluorocarbons changes the molecule, adversely affecting glide. According to Dr. Thanos Karydas of Dominator Waxes, the reason is that under heat, fluoros tend to sublimate, something like evaporating. We began corking-in fluoros at the Thunder Bay World Championships in 1995, and certainly after several minutes of vigorous corking, all fluorocarbon had gone transparent and had definitely gone "into the base."

In 1999 at the Ramsau World Championships, the word was that corking "stretched" the fluoro molecule and was a contributing factor in the speed of a ski.

Corking fluorocarbons should also result in less aerosols—dust—in the air, and thus a higher degree of safety (see the next chapter).

The new felt polishing pads produce heat much more easily than cork does and are proving to be a very useful tool. However, roto-felt tools may provide too much heat, and top waxers prefer to polish with felt by hand or with a roto-cork made of natural materials or plastic/foam.

It has also been suggested that fluorocarbon molecules orient in a more uniform and effective fashion in the presence of high humidity or water.

At Thunder Bay, we tested this by spraying bases with a household atomizer (the kind that contains its own pump and is used for window-cleaning fluid and other products). We would spray the base, brush vigorously, spray again, brush, spray, brush. Bases were all brushed the same amount. Glide test results using this method of application indicated a significant increase in speed, of up to .8 kilometer per hour.

Wet-brushing should result in fewer aerosols, and thus contribute to greater wax room safety. I would conjecture that the presence of water also reduces static buildup.

Finish off fluoro application by brushing.

### Brushing

Dedicate a horsehair brush to fluorocarbons. A brush that has been used for paraffins will only spread a thin layer of paraffin over the fluorocarbon, actually slowing the ski by as much as one or two kilometers per hour. I store my fluoro brushes in their own plastic bags, to keep them clean and separate. It's also a good idea to label your fluoro brush, to avoid confusion when in a hurry (it can be hard to tell a horsehair brush from a nylon brush that has been used in graphite). Roto brushes are nice, especially if you are doing a lot of skis, but not necessary.

Brush thoroughly, wet or dry: the purpose of brushing is to remove all the "bumps," and polish out a thin membrane of fluorocarbon over the base. Brushing will also polish this membrane into the "walls" of the structure.

## Putting Fluoros on Classic Skis

No matter how careful you are about applying and brushing fluorocarbons, if they get into the kick zone of classic skis the results can be disastrous—the fluorocarbon will happily go right on doing what it is supposed to do, which is to provide a surface nothing will stick to, including kick wax.

To avoid rapid loss of kick wax, simply tape the kick zone of your classic skis with masking tape (figure 9) before applying fluoros. After ironing and brushing, remove the masking tape, and the skis are ready for kick wax application. It will be easier to remove the masking tape if you use a size a little wider than the ski. Duct tape is not as good as masking tape, as it tends to leave traces of adhesive which get into the kick wax.

(To get square ends on the tape—actually a help, as it makes ironing easier—tear the tape at the ends of the kick zone against a sharp scraper.)

After removing the tape, there may be a small bump where the fluoro built up during ironing and brushing. Simply wipe this

*Figure 9. Taping the kick wax zone with masking tape, in order to keep fluoros off the base. Note the simple method for making an even cut in the tape.*

away with a piece of Fiberlene. Be sure to wipe *away* from the kick zone.

## Maintenance

Because fluorocarbons last over long distances, it is possible to use the same skis in several shorter races, without applying more. Be sure to keep the skis clean—perhaps travel with them in a plastic sleeve such as the ones they sometimes come in. Before reuse, brush them down with a fluoro (horsehair) brush.

Do not reapply fluoros without rewaxing as well, as you run a chance of "drying out" the base. Some skiers report deteriorating performance when a ski has simply been "waxed" with fluoros over and over. This may be due to drying out, or it may also be due to the base sealing from too much heat.

To remove fluoros, simply wax with a normal paraffin, and scrape. The paraffin will lift the fluoro out of the base.

## Fluoros and Junior Racing

I would like to end the discussion of fluoros with a personal note that I feel strongly about: I believe fluorocarbons are not appropriate to local junior competition. Fluoros are most effective at greater distances than juniors race; they are expensive; their use involves potential health hazards; and for short distances, at any rate, you can often find a paraffin combination that is faster. Use of fluoros in junior competition is too "high-tech," and it distracts from the proper focuses of junior skiing: fun, and learning good technique.

# 14

**Chapter**

# SAFETY IN THE WAX ROOM

Up to this point, we have dealt directly with the whys and hows of waxing. It would be negligent not to take a look at safety issues in the wax room. I am indebted to Dr. Thanos Karydas, of Dominator Waxes, for much of the information in this chapter.

There are three kinds of health hazards involved when dealing with chemicals: oral toxicity, skin irritation, and eye irritation.

Ski waxes are usually classed as "nontoxic," and are not generally skin or eye irritants—though this sidesteps the issue of particles and chips which may lodge in the eyes. But in spite of the nontoxic and nonirritating classification of ski waxes, there are other ways in which substances we use in the wax room can become quite hazardous.

**Do not heat fluoros with an open flame. If you are applying fluoro klisters, USE AN IRON!** Normal hydrocarbons (nonfluorinated waxes) are probably safe. However, a study done by Swedish industrial safety experts in 1989 reported that during ironing, wax vaporizes and then becomes liquid in the form of tiny droplets. These droplets can be inhaled into the lung alveoli and impair lung function.

This research demonstrated that there is a reduction of lung function after exposure to ski wax vapor. The wax technicians observed during the study all showed a decrease in lung function, ranging from 10 to 25 percent, after 5 days of waxing. The technicians showed recovery after rest periods, but the effect was cumulative for the duration of the test. From personal experience

I can attest to severe breathlessness after prolonged waxing in confined, non-ventilated areas.

The Swedish study only included hydrocarbon waxes. Fluorocarbons give off a great deal of vapor when ironed, despite a higher melting point than hydrocarbons. Fluorocarbons are likely to remain in the system longer, since they are not as biodegradable.

Disclaimers on fluorocarbon boxes state that the contents are inert and therefore, presumably, not dangerous—you can eat all of them you want. This begs the issue: fluoros are highly toxic if heated in a flame or if, as happened to one Finnish coach, they drift onto a burning cigarette. In these cases, fluoros can be lethal.

Be sure to wax at a low enough temperature that your iron does not smoke! Smoking irons can release dangerous chemicals and aerosols into the air. If there are a lot of smoking irons in the wax room, leave—or wear a mask.

It's also good to keep in mind that we are always learning more about the chemicals we use. Many chemicals that were once considered safe are now no longer allowed in household products. Some of the waxes (and wax removers) that are common in the wax room may still be shown to be dangerous. It is wise to exercise as much caution as possible.

What can be done?

- Always wax in a well-ventilated area.
- Avoid ironing at temperatures much above the minimum needed (which will also be good for the base).
- If another waxer's iron is smoking, get him to turn it down to a lower setting.
- Leave the area if the smoke and vapor are too much.
- Wear a mask or respirator.
- Encourage your club to add ventilation in the waxing area.
- Never wax with an open flame.

In addition to the hazardous effects of heating waxes and fluoros, there is the more subtle danger of dust.

Brushing fluorocarbons puts an enormous amount of dust in the air. Several years ago, while working at a World Cup in Lahti,

I was in the wax room finishing several pairs of skis that we had "waxed" with fluoros. As the afternoon wore on, the sun came through the window at a low angle, illuminating the dust in the air. I was staggered by the amount of tiny particles in suspension in the air we were breathing. And with the advent of roto brushes, even "normal" hydrocarbon waxes are putting a great deal of particulate matter into the air. Use that respirator!

Also be aware of the particles that roto brushes can throw into your eyes.

**15**

# WAX ROOMS AND TEST AREAS

Waxing is as much a part of skiing as training or racing, yet it always seems to come as a complete surprise to race organizers and club officials that skiers need wax rooms and a place to test skis.

Good waxing and wax testing facilities at a club or race site will help to avoid problems during racing and training, and will enhance trail/area facilities in general.

## The Wax Room

Waxing areas should be located as close as possible to the start area, and with good, quick access to the trails.

Applying glide wax and working on bases is always best done indoors, and it is often necessary to apply kick wax at the last moment. Providing a covered, warm area for doing this can make waxing much easier, and having the waxing area close to the starting area will be a real plus.

A good wax room will include most, if not all, of the following:

- Heat.
- Good lighting, with light sources located directly above permanent wax benches.
- Plenty of power outlets, located conveniently to the benches. The more sockets, the better.
- Good ventilation. This is a very real health concern. Many teams and shops are installing hoods over their wax tables, with fans to draw out smoke, aerosols, etc.
- Floors that are easy to clean (concrete).
- Nonskid floors, which allow skis to be leaned against

the walls without sliding out. Carpeting can be laid around the outer edge of the room, to a width of about 18 inches from the wall, so that skis can be based on the carpeting, while leaving the rest of the floor uncarpeted (cement) for easy cleaning.

- Wall racks of some kind: Skiers will need to lean skis against the wall, and some sort of rack will go a long way toward eliminating the "domino effect."
- Overhead storage. This will decongest the walls. A set of 2-by-4-inch planks hung about 8 inches from the ceiling will provide excellent storage for skis not immediately in use.
- Possible additional storage area for ski bags, etc.
- Separate waxing facilities for different teams can be a real plus.
- Some lockers for warm-ups, clothing changes, etc.

Once a club or touring area has outfitted a well-organized wax room, the next goal should be to set up a testing area where skiers can test waxes and skis. This will be an advantage for any permanent site: a convenient and well-laid-out testing area will encourage racers and coaches to include testing as an important part of the whole art of cross-country skiing. (Specific test methods are covered in Chapters 16 and 17.)

## Testing and Warm-up Areas

### For Kick Wax

The best place to test kick wax is out on the training or race trail. If starting fields are small, so that all racers can start reasonably close to the same time, it will usually be no problem for skiers and coaches to test wax on the trail.

But if there is a large field, or multiple classes and start times, it will be necessary for later starters to be able to go on testing wax and warming up. In these cases, it may be possible to continue to permit coaches and racers on the actual ski course, but this can lead to interference with racers. If this is the case, the usual procedure is to close the course 15 minutes before the first start.

If it is necessary to close the course in this way, it is essential to provide alternate warm-up and wax-testing tracks. If the weather is changing, ongoing wax testing is vital, and of course, athletes will need to warm up for later starts. Such alternate tracks must be as close as possible to the starting and waxing areas. They should be long enough for sufficient testing and warm-up, with suitable terrain including uphills and downhills.

Test warm-up tracks must be treated *exactly* the same as the race course! This means the tracks must be groomed and set at the same time, in the same way, with the same machinery. If there is going to be more than one day of racing, they should be regroomed and reset daily.

On the test tracks, the uphills should be steep enough and long enough for athletes to get the feel for their skis and their technique, and downhills should be long enough to permit some glide testing.

### For Glide Wax and Skis

As in kick wax testing, the best place to test glide wax and skis is on the race track. In many cases, it will be possible to allow testing on the tracks up to 15 minutes before the start. However, there are several reasons why this may not be possible:

- No suitable terrain (described below) is available.
- There is ongoing racing on the track.
- Too many teams are testing on the track, causing interference with skiers using the course for training or racing.
- Testing with a speed trap has resulted in creating a "stopping berm" at the end of the testing area, or in erasing a possible second track by skiing back up the test hill.

If any of these reasons pertain, it is a very good idea to create a separate wax/ski testing area, consisting of a test hill with tracks down it. A separate test area is provided at top-level races. Such an area should meet the following criteria:

- The testing area must be as close as possible to the waxing area and the start, with as much protection from the wind as possible.

- It should be at least 50 meters long, with sufficient run-out to allow skiers to glide skis out to a stop (longer is better).
- The hill should allow skiers to reach speeds of 15 to 25 kilometers per hour.
- There should be a sufficient number of parallel tracks for all teams to test on, with enough room between them so that skiers in adjacent tracks will not interfere with each other.
- There should be room between parallel tracks to permit a standing place for a person operating a speed trap (see Chapter 16).
- The test tracks should include a good path for returning to the top of the test hill; this can be around to one side, or between every two to four sets of tracks. Be sure that such an up track is wide enough to permit comfortable skating.

A workable alternative is to widen part of the regular trail (on a long, straight hill) and set test tracks to the side of the race track. This section of the trail should be fenced or flagged off from the course, to avoid interfering with racers. The same need for an "up track" pertains, as above.

A club or touring area with good waxing and testing facilities is providing a very positive service to the skiing community. We need full-service skiing areas that not only enhance the cross-country experience, but also promote continued learning and experimentation.

# 16
**Chapter**

# TESTING SKIS AND GLIDE

Wax and ski testing are complex subjects, and much that passes for "testing" gives no reliable data. On the other hand, an understanding of testing methods will help any skier to make more intelligent choices about equipment and wax.

In order to be reliable, testing has to be as simple as possible. In this chapter we will examine a number of different testing procedures, from the very simple to the kind of testing that will be available only to teams or skiers who can invest in some rather expensive equipment. The goal, however, will be to come back to a few simple methods that will be of use to anyone interested in doing basic testing.

**The first rule of testing: Eliminate variables.** This is essential for accurate, meaningful results. Eliminating variables means that for wax testing, the camber, brand, and structure must match. For structure testing, camber, brand, and wax must match. And for ski testing, structure and wax must match.

Let's look at the four common types of testing: speed traps, glideout tests, "competitive" glide testing, and subjective testing.

## Speed Traps

The most "scientific" testing method is to use a speed trap: generally, you ski through a light beam which starts a clock, glide a given distance, then ski through another light beam which stops the clock. Recently a number of less expensive, simpler speed trap systems have come on the market. These consist of a device worn on your leg which detects when you pass a magnet on a post planted in the snow.

Problems that can affect this method are:
- wind
- changes in the track due to skiing or falling snow
- wax abrasion
- unevenness of the track: curves, bumps
- unevenness of the start
- boot covers (these can rub the wall of the track, slowing the ski)
- the snow in the track may not correlate to the snow out of the track, as in skating (see below)
- uneven riding of the skis from run to run

The speed trap method is unsuitable for ski selection (covered later in this chapter), but it does have the following advantages:
- objective and recordable times/speeds
- the test can be done at skiing speeds
- many pairs/waxes can be tested in a short time
- suitable for wax and structure selection

Be aware that a large margin of error is possible in this method. Variations from run to run of up to .1 kilometer per hour are common, and can be much larger. In fact, the variations within a set of runs on one ski will often be larger than the difference between the average runs of two pairs. This calls into question the validity of the process, but keeping careful records will allow long-term patterns to emerge; these are the most important data.

Speed trap tests made out of a track allow a myriad of additional variables to enter in—it is simply impossible to ski the same way on each pair without a track—and in my experience produce results with such a wide spread of data as to be useless.

**The second rule of testing: Keep records!** (For a sample test sheet, see Appendix 3.)

## Glide-out Tests

The most common and easiest test method is to glide the skis out from a common starting point, and see which glides farthest, but the problems with this method include all of those mentioned under speed trap testing, plus the fact that at the crucial, final part of the glide-out, speed is far below skiing speed. The smallest varia-tions of wind, weighting, etc. can make a tremendous difference in results where speed and momentum are at their lowest. In ad-dition, glide-out testing makes quantification of data impossible.

The main advantage of glide-out testing is its simplicity, and it can also be somewhat useful for ski selection.

### "Competitive" Glide Testing

Both of the first two methods discussed above assume that the same skier is doing all the gliding. But a third method is also com-mon, what we might call "competitive" glide testing, where two skiers see who glides farther or accelerates the fastest. A good way to do this is for the skiers to stand beside each other and then, holding hands to equalize starting speed, begin to glide down the track. They should release hands when an even start has been ac-complished, and see which ski accelerates the fastest and/or glides the farthest.

There are problems with this method as well:

- Skiers of different weights will produce different results: weight affects pressure distribution, and hence acceleration and glide; a heavier skier will tend to gather more momentum and glide farther.
- Commonly, different skiers will be on different ski brands, or have different structure.
- Different skiers weight skis differently (forward or back, riding edges), affecting glide and acceleration.
- "Competitive" glide testing is not suited to testing multiple pairs.
- Quantification of data is impossible.

Some of these problems can be eliminated by switching skis back and forth between skiers.

A serious problem that is common to all the above methods must be understood: When skiing, you weight your skis with full body weight or more while gliding. For example, in classic cross-country skiing, you glide with full body weight on one ski. While skating, you can weight the gliding ski with several times your body weight, as you prepare the next stride. By contrast, all glide testing is done at 50 percent of body weight (that is, weight is evenly distributed onto both skis). Thus, all the above testing methods give data on glide under conditions different from actual skiing!

Glide tests are best used to select wax or structure. Another method must be used for ski selection. This is "subjective testing."

## Subjective Testing

Although glide-out testing (the second method) can be used for ski selection, the most effective method for this is subjective testing. It is also a good way to test wax. Subjective testing is done in two ways: Either by skiing with one ski from pair "A" on one foot, and one ski from pair "B" on the other foot, to compare "breaking" speed/feel and whether the skis stall on uphills; or by skiing a short loop on one pair, changing pairs, and repeating the loop.

Subjective testing takes practice, so it should be an ongoing, integral part of training, whether the goal is to test skis or wax. Skiers have to know their skis well, and the skills gained from this kind of testing are invaluable.

Good skiers can compare skis very accurately. I once had Bill Koch rate six pairs this way. I had just tested the same skis through the speed trap, and Bill was able to rank them exactly the same way I had done with my instruments.

Torgney Magren was doing very valuable and accurate testing by feel during the 1999 World Championships, in conditions where wind and falling snow made other types of testing impossible—another good reason to cultivate a feel for your skis.

## Simple Testing Options

How does the private skier, or even the average team, test? Assuming that buying a speed trap is not an option, I would suggest the following:

### Testing Wax/Structure

Wax testing is not all that important: all modern brands are good, and if you read the labels and have air and snow thermometers, and possibly a hygrometer, you won't go far astray.

If you want to test wax or structure, use the glide-out or the "competitive" method, but be sure to eliminate the variables. Be sure you have a good track, and that you run out on flats: hitting an uphill makes it very difficult to see any meaningful differences.

Don't try to test small variations in wax, or too many waxes at once. Test between brands, or between whole colors (as opposed to mixes), to try to amplify differences so they will be meaningful.

Don't try to test waxes on unmatched skis. I often see someone testing different waxes on a pair of Fischers, a pair of Karhus, a pair of Rossignols, and maybe a pair of Madshus. What do the results show? Which flex was best? Which structure was best? What base material was fastest? The chances of successfully identifying the best wax this way are close to nil. Moral? Be logical, only test one thing at a time, and have a plan. Eliminate variables, and keep it simple!

One final note: When wax testing, be sure to number the skis, and record what wax is on each one! Put duct tape patches on the tips, number these with a marker pen, and record everything.

### Ski Selection

Learn to select skis by feel: at the top international level, it is common for racers to ignore the speed trap altogether, and select their skis based on actual performance. It is better to ski on a pair of skis that are working for you on uphills, than on a pair that are perhaps a little faster on downhills. Many successful skiers will race on a pair of skis that is maybe third fastest in the speed trap, but has the best feel on the uphills. Again, remember, you spend some 70 percent of your time climbing.

Testing for the best classic pair is different from testing for the best skating pair. Here is the protocol:

**Classic skis.** Wax one ski from each pair, or wax all the possible skis, and wax them all the same. Go ski a short loop, being sure to ski an uphill. Try to feel glide, but above all, notice which kicks best. Pick the ski that helps you up the hill the most. Kick wax testing will be discussed in detail in Chapter 17.

**Skating skis.** Again, wax all your skis the same, then ski on one ski from each pair, or alternate pairs. Notice glide, but also be careful to note how the skis act uphill, when you are weighting them hard. If the ski helps you up the hill, it's the one to pick.

Conversely, if it "dies" on the uphill, pick the other ski.

Record all results. Developing a database takes time and work, but will produce valuable information that will simplify arriving at good skis.

## Instruments

At least two thermometers are needed in the waxer's equipment box, as well as a hygrometer.

### Thermometers

I prefer a digital model, as these are easier to read. But just because a thermometer is digital, it is not necessarily accurate! My digital thermometers have varied by as much as 3° from each other, and the same will be seen in many readily available mercury thermometers. To keep records straight, it is best to designate which thermometer is used for which purpose, and accept that as a standard. Note, however, that the temperature range of most modern kick and glide waxes is quite wide, and the current tendency is to widen even further. Thus, being off by a degree or so will have little impact on wax selection, and especially in the case of kick wax, *careful, personal testing* is the only reliable way to find a wax (more on testing procedures later).

If you have a digital thermometer, ignore the tenths: round temperatures (and humidity) to the nearest whole number. You do not need to rewax because the temperature has just gone up .2°!

### Hygrometers

For measuring humidity I prefer a digital, electronic hygrometer, but some models of these will not work in colder temperatures. Filament, or dial, hygrometers are controlled by the stretching/shrinking of a hair filament. While cheaper than the digital instruments, they need frequent adjustment, the hair can age, and they can be slow to react—and, like some digital versions, they may not work in colder temperatures.

A hygrometer can be calibrated by wrapping it in a wet towel, then adjusting it to read 100 percent.

## Advanced Glide Testing

I am indebted to Finnish Head Coach Antti Leppävuori for suggesting many of the following ideas.

The most careful testing includes first the calibration of the test skis with the same wax, then waxing all pairs differently and one pair similarly to the calibration ("0 pair"), and testing them again.

The testing place should be calm (no wind; even the slightest wind will cause trouble). Make at least six test runs for each pair. Count averages, standard deviation, and trend. Averages are the main result of possible differences, standard deviation indicates the accuracy of the test skier and conditions (wind), and trend indicates changes in the track. (Near 0°C, changes caused by the track can be very strong.)

A whole test may include sixty runs altogether—a pretty big job, but pretty reliable, too. Differences over 1 percent from the average of the 0 pair are significant. If the differences in the calibration and in the wax test are smaller than 1 percent, you can presume that there are no differences between the waxes.

Skis are sometimes faster on the first test run, and get slower after that. This acceleration might be due to dirt or water, as well as to hard ice crystals, which wear the ski base and wax. At first the bases are smooth, and glide better, but after each run, more "scratches" get into the base, and the ski slows down. In these conditions, pay attention to changes in the trend to get information on the properties of the wax.

The test skier is very important. If you have several skiers testing with the same test pairs, you can get confused data. Skiers have different kinds of "touch" with the skis, and even small changes in weight or balance can cause changes in the pressure distribution of the skis. Test with one test skier.

The problem of subjective versus objective testing is an eternal question. Try to exclude big differences with objective tests, and small differences with "touch," or subjective tests.

When testing kick wax, pay more attention to good kick than to glide.

Glide and kick on diagonal (classic) skis is more a question of the camber than the wax itself. Even though the wax manufacturers claim that the glide of the kick wax is essential, don't put too much importance on this. Instead, remember that the function of the kick wax is to *kick,* not to glide. The glide comes from other things (glide wax, pressure distribution).

All this is ideal. In a competition situation, the procedures have to be simplified. Even then, don't accept differences smaller than 1 percent, the practical "limit of UME" (unrecognized measuring errors).

## Other Methods

Some teams, notably the Italians, test with a series of speed traps, which allows them to test the acceleration rate of the skis.

Some years ago, work was being done on a small roller or paddle wheel that would attach to the tail of the ski. This connected to a small computer, and recorded the speed and acceleration rate of the ski, which could be graphed. This excellent concept never made it off the ground, but seemed, and still seems, remarkably useful.

The Russians produced the "egg beater," a small machine that rotates P-Tex discs against the snow, and measures resistance. This allows the technician to test as many waxes as he has discs, in a quick, recordable fashion. It also allows the technician to test waxes in various areas (high point, low point, etc.) in a very short time.

Some work has also been done on a device that would pull a ski along a rail, measuring resistance.

All of these methods are attempts to assemble objective, recordable data using a method that is simple and easily portable. Eliminating the variations due to the skier (uneven weighting of the ski, air resistance, etc.) are also highly desirable.

I should add that Jim Galanes and I made a conscious decision not to calibrate skis, once they had been shown to be reasonably uniform: the adjustments we were making through calibration were more precise than the tolerances of the testing method, and thus were meaningless. To quote Karl Popper, " . . . it is always undesirable to make an effort to increase precision for its own sake. . . . One should never be more precise than the problem situation demands."

**17**

# TESTING KICK WAX

The simplest and most logical way to test kick wax is by what I'll call the "split-pair" system. This system is very logical, and often does not take a great deal of time. In its more complex form, for multiple skiers, it was developed by Jim Galanes for the Val di Fiemme World Championship season.

A pair of classic skis is assumed—a pair that you know and can rely on for the feel of the wax.

If you can, take a wax bench out on the course in an area of "typical snow," so that testing can be done where it matters, without wasting time skiing back to the wax room. This will also remove you from the general panic- and rumor-stricken atmosphere of the waxing area, and will allow for much more objective testing.

Write it down: Put duct tape or masking tape on the test skis, and mark each one with notes as to what wax is being applied. Or mark the skis "A" and "B" in large, clear letters, and write the waxes down on a piece of paper. If you don't write it down, you'll forget which one was which.

A sample test form for split-pair testing is provided in Appendix 3.

## Preparation

Your wax station should have (ideally):

- a portable table and/or a form bench
- wax supply (including improbable waxes—weather can change)

- thermometers
- a hygrometer
- corks
- putty knives for stripping wax
- a blowtorch and lighter
- Fiberlene and wax remover (using wax remover will make applying another wax very difficult)
- "hairy" tools and silicone
- a notebook for recording test results

To begin, check the thermometer, the humidity, and the state of the track (packed, new, etc.), and make a ball-park choice of wax. Try to guess whether binder will be needed.

If binder seems to be needed, apply it to one ski; then apply the ball-park wax to both skis. Go ski, and put in as much distance as you can. When you come back in, check to see if the ski with binder has appreciably more wax left, and make your decision as to whether it is needed or not. If you have more than one skier working with you, send one out to test binder, while you, and any others, concentrate on kick wax.

If binder is not needed, proceed straight to kick wax testing.

## Testing Basics

Apply the ball-park wax to one ski, then apply another wax to the other ski. Go ski, and feel which wax is working better. There are two considerations in testing kick wax: kick and glide.

**Kick.** Be sure to test the wax on uphills, and in areas where the snow may be different, such as shaded spots, in direct sun, and on the back side of the hill.

Include some tests at race-pace; how the wax does when you're out walking the dog does not necessarily indicate how it will do when you have to turn it on. Then try skiing badly: if a wax is kicking very well, it should tolerate a little deliberate late kicking and/or weak kick. Remember, when the race is on, the skier is going to become tired, and technique will suffer.

Record kick on a 1-to-5 scale, with 1 as bad and 5 as perfect, a "roller ski kick."

**Glide.** Feel the ski: Does it break easily? Does it glide long? Can you feel any drag? Is it fast, free? Feel the skis on uphills as well as flats.

Record glide on a 1-to-5 scale, with 1 as bad and 5 as perfect.

## Rate and Retest

Continue to rate and retest waxes until you have good kick and glide. To do this, *retain the best wax from each test,* strip the other ski, and rewax it. Repeat the test procedure with the new wax. This way, you always have a reference point; changing the wax on both skis at the same time leaves you with no comparison available.

**Strip the ski thoroughly** between tests: if you are testing a new wax on top of a layer of old wax, what worked? Strip the base with a putty knife or spatula, or with a blowtorch and Fiberlene—but not with wax remover unless absolutely necessary.

Always test with as few variables at one time as possible.

When you are close to good wax, you may wish to refine the kick, but be sure you change only one wax at a time, so that you have a reference point.

**To improve kick,** you should:

- thicken the wax for more kick
- lengthen the wax for more kick
- add a layer of something softer (or harder) for more kick
- add a layer of graphite or fluorocarbon wax for better glide

Memorize the acronym TLS: Thicker, Longer, Softer: always add more kick by changing the wax in this order.

**If you have more skiers available**, wax testing can encompass far more testing in a very short time. Here is the system:

- All skiers must be in contact either by radio, or by reporting back to a base area at a set time.
- All skiers must have a common wax for a reference point—say, extra-blue.
- All results should be compared and recorded on the 1-to-5 scale.

- Someone must be designated to record results. Be sure to record whose results each set of numbers are. Also record time.
- All waxes should be applied as alike as possible—that is, similar amounts, same number of layers, equally well corked.

Skiers should use as closely matched skis as possible, or know whose skis are stiffer, who usually needs more kick, etc.

As long as everyone uses the same common wax on one ski, so that all share a common reference, you can test as many different waxes as you have skiers. The more skiers you have, the more waxes you can input into the test, and because everyone was comparing to the same common wax, comparisons between the different waxes can be made.

If time permits, everyone can go out for a second or third test, using the common wax or selecting a new common wax on the basis of the first test. In a short time, a great many combinations can be tested.

This system takes some practice, but in two or three well-planned sessions, everyone involved will get a feel for it, and gain confidence. The system should be part of training, and of ongoing wax testing as new waxes are introduced. In fact, every training session should to some degree be a testing session as well. Through ongoing, systematic testing, you will quickly gain much solid information about a broad range of waxes. You will also gain much more "feel" for your skis, and all this will boost your confidence in your preparations and equipment.

# SKI REPAIR

Ski repair may seem to be off the beaten path from the rest of this book, but sooner or later skis will get damaged, and suddenly repair work becomes very much a part of ski preparation.

Generally, damage is more psychological than actual: a scratch or two can often be more or less ignored, and there are battle-scarred skis that are still very fast, even at the international level. In fact, damaged skis are almost more common at the international level because of two things: top racers know a good pair when they have them, and they hang on to them; and top racers are often more focused on going out and skiing fast than many citizen racers, who tend to obsess over minutiae and details.

The amount of friction caused by a scratch or two doesn't have much of an effect on glide; the real enemies are bad bases (burned or scraped badly), and even more important, the wrong skis for the skier and/or the conditions. Know your skis, and never give up on a good pair!

## Bindings

It's pretty important to keep bindings securely attached! An ounce of prevention may prevent them from loosening or tearing out.

### Mounting Bindings

If the skis are new, make sure they're mounted properly:

- Use the approved jig or paper outline (properly placed; read the instructions) when you install your bindings.
- Drill binding holes with the proper-size drill, to the recommended depth. Buying a binding screw drill is a

good investment. These are designed to cut only to the correct depth, and are the right diameter. Be sure the hole is deep enough: some thinner skis will show bumps under the binding screws, where the screw has pushed core material or glue down against the base.

- Tap the hole with a thread cutter, if you can find one. This makes screws go in much more easily, and as it cuts threads, rather than allowing them to be "crushed in," it makes for a better "hold." You can also tap the holes for the "heel plates," as this gives the little fins on the pins something to grab.

- Work some glue into the holes. You can use epoxy (slow-cure glues allow you more working time), but a common white glue will also work. The purpose of the glue is as much to seal the hole against moisture as it is to hold the screw, so a lot of glue is not needed. (Epoxy glues will flow better if you preheat the individual epoxy tubes under hot water—but note that this makes the glue set faster, which can be a problem with fast-set epoxies. Hot glues can also used, but work fast—hot glues set up quickly!)

- You can also glue-in heel plates, etc. A little epoxy on the pin that secures the heel plate can prevent disaster.

- The "strip away" patches on heel plates hold better if the ski and binding are gently heated with a heat gun. It can also be a good idea to rough up the top plate of the ski slightly, so the patches can hold better; be sure there is no dirt on the surface, as this will loosen the adhesive. "Set" the heel plates by rubbing something solid up and down over the area with the patches; if the glue isn't set at installation, it may never have a chance to take hold after water has gotten under the heel plate.

### Loose or Torn-out Bindings

If a binding pulls out, allow the hole to dry thoroughly. If the hole from the ripped-out binding is small enough to hold the screw, fill the hole with epoxy (work it in with a matchstick), and screw the binding back on; be careful not to pull it down too tight, as this can strip what is left of the core or top sheet. Allow the epoxy ample time to set: this is now all that is holding the binding on.

If the hole is too big to take hold of the screw, fill the hole with glue and some kind of plug (steel wool, a matchstick, etc.), allow it to cure, then redrill the hole, and start over from the beginning by tapping, and then gluing, the binding screws in.

Or, you can simply push a rolled-up bit of steel wool into the glue-filled hole, and then put the screw into the hole and snug it down—but work fast, before the glue hardens. Be sure to allow ample curing time for the glue.

If the hole is really big, you can fill it, move the binding backwards or forwards a few millimeters, and never know the difference.

Bindings themselves are much harder, and usually impossible, to repair. Don't depend on a broken or repaired binding, unless it's just a case of replacing a part.

## Scratches

Although less aggressive scratches can be rounded out with sandpaper and Fibertex, or by grinding, really bad scratches—gouges—can be filled.

### Filling Gouges

Begin by cleaning the whole area very thoroughly: repairs will not adhere to a waxed base. Clean the base with wax remover, and wipe clean. Then sand the scratch with a medium-grit paper (the actual size is not important); this cleans the area more, but the real purpose is to rough up the area so that the repair will stick.

There are now two ways to proceed: with a P-Tex stick (or "candle"), or with epoxy.

**With epoxy**, choose a slow-cure type. I prefer the black-and-white "metal repair" epoxies, as these set up well for later shaping. They are good on bases, and they work for sidewalls and edges as well.

Epoxy will adhere better to the base material if you quickly and carefully pass a blowtorch over the area to be glued; this oxidizes the P-Tex of the base, allowing a better glue-to-base bond.

Then simply mix the epoxy, apply, and allow it to harden thoroughly, probably for 24 hours.

**With P-Tex sticks,** begin by getting a good repair stick, in the right color for your base (color isn't important, but the right color looks a lot better). I prefer the long, round sticks used by repair shops, as these are a better type of P-Tex altogether, but the regular round ones, somewhat smaller, will do almost as well.

Preheat the afflicted area with a heat gun, or with a blowtorch. Do this *very* carefully; too much will fry the base and close the pores, but the P-Tex patch will adhere better if the area it goes onto is warm. Now heat the P-Tex stick with a propane torch: if you "bury" the stick in the flame, it will help keep the stick from burning and getting blobs of soot into the repair. Keeping the flame near the base (but not too near—use with discretion!) will help keep the base warm, and help adhesion. Allow the P-Tex from the stick to flow into the scratch. Turn off the torch, and go do something else; the patch needs time to cool thoroughly.

Once the patch is cooled, scrape the bump it will leave with a very sharp steel scraper, using gentle, fast motions: don't try to take it all off at once! This may leave a dimple on the ski (especially on an edge), and it is usually necessary to repeat the process several times, building up a little more new base each time. It takes time, but with patience you can make a repair that will be virtually invisible.

Edges are more difficult. You can form a "dam" with a steel scraper and a clamp, and flow the P-Tex in between the dam and the scraper, but I prefer to do it as outlined above, bit by bit.

The best way of all to do base repairs is with a P-Tex repair gun. A glue gun will not work: the good, big sticks won't fit, and the heat is not enough. There are also "soldering iron" P-Tex heaters, which work like a flattened soldering iron: with these you "smear" the P-Tex into the base for a good bond. But the gun is the best way to go, if you can afford one, because they actually force the new P-Tex into the pores of the old, for a very good bond.

One word of caution: Neither glue nor P-Tex sticks will hold wax, because the repair material they leave is not porous. For this reason, I very rarely do the kind of repair outlined above. Simply minimize the damage by rounding it out with sandpaper or by steel-scraping or stone-grinding.

### Not-So-Bad Scratches

These can usually be ignored. Especially if they're along the line of travel, they won't make much difference at all. Sand them with a fine sandpaper as much as is needed to take the edge off the scratch, then use Fibertex, or steel-scrape the area with a sharp scraper. Finish by rewaxing.

Cut "hang-nails" off the edges with a knife.

## Delamination

Older skis used to delaminate at the tail very easily. This is no longer so common, as gluing techniques have improved, but I still see it from time to time, and also tip delamination. Try to stop these as soon as they appear—they can get worse fast. Delamination can occur between the top sheet and the core, or between the base and the core. Usually this is easy to fix, and a good repair job will leave the ski as good as new.

The skis should be allowed to dry completely. This will often be best accomplished by propping the delamination open with a matchstick or something of the sort. Let it sit overnight.

Without peeling the delamination any further, sand both surfaces with a clean piece of medium-grit sandpaper. If you are dealing with base material, pass the P-Tex through the flame of a propane torch to oxidize it for better bonding. Apply slow-cure epoxy to the area, and clamp. You can use either a cork or a steel scraper to hold the clamped area flat, if the tip of your clamp is smaller than the area being worked on.

Do not clamp tightly; this will squirt the epoxy out, and a certain amount of it is needed to make the bond. Allow to sit overnight. Remove the clamp(s) and scrapers or corks, and sand away any epoxy that has flowed out. If you find epoxy on the base, sand lightly, and scrape, then rewax.

Note: If the scraper or cork is bonded to the ski, take it off with a quick, light pop with a hammer or some other heavy object; it will come off cleanly this way.

## Bubbles

Bubbles in the base are caused when too much heat is applied to the base in ironing, and/or if the base has not been properly glued. These are hard to deal with, but there are three alternatives:

- Ignore them. If they are small enough, their effect will be so little as to make no difference.
- Apply heat, then clamp (gently). When the area has cooled and the clamp is removed, the bump may stay down . . . but it probably won't.
- If the bump won't stay down, it may be time for surgery: cut a slit at one corner of the bump, work slow-cure epoxy in, block and/or clamp, and allow to set. Sand and scrape overflow epoxy.

## Dents

Dents can happen in travel, when the ski bag is banged or bindings dig into the base, or when the people at the airline whose job it is to drop, pound, and throw your baggage around are really enthusiastic about their job. Dents can also happen if you clamp a delamination too hard.

Dents usually can't be filled, but they rarely do any serious damage to glide. Ignore them, and scrape glide wax out by bending the blade of your plastic scraper.

In summary, if it works, don't fix it!

# APPENDIX 1

# TOOL LIST

What follows is not definitive, but is an overview of tools needed for all the operations outlined in the previous chapters, along with a brief description of use in some cases. The list is alphabetical; the tools I believe to be absolute necessities are in bold print.

**Blowtorch.** For outdoor wax application, heating non-electric irons, and some repair work. The new self-lighting torches are wonderful: they are convenient, you don't have to worry about wet matches or sparkers that don't work, and they save gas. Get one. Propane works much better than butane, but note that U.S. torch heads will not work on European gas cans. Propane canisters are illegal to carry on the plane, so if you're going to Europe, plan on buying a torch there. In Scandinavia, it is still possible to get propane torches; in Central Europe, butane seems to have taken over.

**Bronze brush.** For base work, very light texturing, opening texture or pores, final prepping with very hard waxes and/or in cold weather, holding Fibertex or stripping pads. As with all brushes, those 2- or 3-inch-long brushes are too small to be used easily; get the big ones.

Burnisher. For burnishing a steel scraper—that is, pulling a wire edge over. Some very good technicians can work wonders with a burnished scraper.

Calculator. For averaging times in wax testing, figuring height/ski length ratios.

**C-clamps, or expandable furniture clamps.** For holding ski benches to tables, repair work. Swix and Toko ski clamps are great for holding form benches in place, but do not offer enough support for some kinds of work if used alone, without a form bench.

Clipboard or notebook, paper, pencils. For note-taking when ski testing. Pencils are much better than pens; pens freeze.

Contact cement. Multiple uses, including repairs.

**Corks.** Foam corks work better; avoid "cork corks." Foam/plastic corks create friction-generated heat sooner, which is what makes the wax smooth out, and they tend to hold together better.

Dropcloths. For waxing installations. A large ski bag can double as a dropcloth. Plastic dropcloths or light tarps are best, as they are lighter and easier to carry.

**Duct tape.** Application unlimited; use for labeling skis when testing. "Without duct tape, skiing would be impossible."

Electric drill. For mounting bindings and adding structural alterations like shelving to wax rooms, with screwdriver bits. Also for use with roto brushes, but be sure it's either a plug-in model or the most powerful battery-driven drill you can find. A fast charger and extra batteries are a must for multiple pairs if you are using a battery-powered drill.

**Epoxy.** Slow-setting epoxies tend to be stronger and give you more time to work. For repairs; many uses.

**Extension cord.** Long, with multiple outlets.

**Felt pen/marker pen.** For marking skis when testing.

**Fiberlene, or very sturdy paper towels.** For cleaning skis after using wax remover.

**Fibertex, Omniprep pads, or 3M Heavy Duty Stripping Pads.** For removing hair from bases; also for repairing damaged edges.

File. Medium-coarse. For sharpening plastic scrapers—or better still, try to find the Toko ceramic scraper sharpener, which does a better job than any file or sandpaper. Keep files in a sleeve, to avoid rust.

Food and drink. Seriously, if you are spending all day in the wax room, the way service people tend to, bring along something to keep your energy up.

**Form bench.** For holding skis when you work on them.

**Hammer.** For all kinds of uses; always keep a small hammer in your wax box.

Hand cleaner. For cleaning klisters or wax residues off your hands. Most wax companies produce a hand cleaner.

**Horsehair brush.** For exclusive use with fluorocarbons. Keep in a separate, clean bag; never use on paraffins. Horsehair is also good for final polishing of hydrocarbons, but be sure it is clearly labeled "paraffin."

Hot-air gun. For use applying binders, waxes, and klisters; also useful for ski cleaning, and for repair work. The two-temperature models are best (use the hotter temperature); ones with sliding heat controls tend to get broken more easily.

Hot-melt glue gun, with appropriate glue. For general repairs and/ or "fixing" binding screws into their holes.

Hygrometer. For measuring air humidity.

**Iron.** For ironing-in wax. Large, hole-less if possible; travel irons should be banned from the wax room, owing to their large temperature fluctuations. Be aware that European voltage is 220; in Europe, buy a new iron. Most of the major wax manufacturers market good waxing irons, and these are much better than the household variety. Some irons have the temperature marked on the temperature control dial, which is very useful; others merely have numbers.

**Klister spreaders/groove scrapers.** For spreading out klister if you prefer not to use your thumb; for wax removal; and for taking the glide wax out of grooves. You can never have too many of these.

Magnifying glass, loupe, or small microscope. For studying the ski base, effect of work at hand; a very useful learning device. Try for magnification of at least 24x.

**Nylon brush.** Always use large brushes, which are easier to handle than the small ones.

**Plastic scraper(s).** For scraping ironed-in wax. Also for repairs.

**P-Tex sticks.** For repairs and modifications of the base. Preferably the long, round sticks used by repair shops, in the right color for your base.

**Putty knife/spatula.** For removing kick wax, klisters; absolutely necessary for stripping skis when wax testing. Bevel slightly with a whetstone, so it can get under the wax.

**Respirator.** For protection when applying fluoros. Use with a filter suitable for organic vapor, hydrochloric acid, and sulfur dioxide, or at least a filter good enough to keep out very small aerosols. Get the kids used to using these!

**Rillers, or rilling bars.** For structuring the base. Assorted "sizes": .5-millimeter, .75-millimeter, 1.0-millimeter, and 3-millimeter cutters are the most useful.

Roto brushes. I use two horsehair brushes (one for paraffins, one for fluoros), a nylon all-purpose brush, and a combi brush. Special Fibertex holders are also great. We are also seeing the advent of the roto cork for fluoro application. Don't get too caught up in the bewildering range of "special" roto brushes.

Sanding block. Wood, to back sandpaper or scraper, or to guide buffing pad.

Sandpaper. To smooth the base. Preferably wet-and-dry or 3M Imperial Microfinish; 80/100, 150, 220, 320, 400 grits. Also for edges, for which 220 is about right.

Scalpel or knife. For everything from opening things to trimming glue buildups, to cleaning up a damaged edge.

Spare binding screws. For replacement or repairs.

**Screwdrivers.** For mounting/removing bindings. Posi-drive and "normal." Ratcheting screwdrivers are great, or if you do a lot of skis, get drivers that you can use in an electric drill.

Speed trap. For testing ski and wax gliding speeds.

Steel brush. For texturing.

**Steel scraper.** For flattening and smoothing the base; also for repairs. Keep in a sleeve to protect the edge (and things around it), and to keep it from rusting. The cobalt steel scrapers are the best available.

Tape player or radio. I always try to keep a little music going in the wax room when I know it's going to be a long session. Honestly, it helps!

Test forms. For wax test recording.

**Thermometers.** For both snow and air. Digital thermometers are easier to read, but be sure you have one that will work cold enough. Try to find one without tenths, as that gets into being overexact.

**Wax remover.** I prefer the less-toxic citrus-based removers. Most wax producers also have a good wax remover. Removers are mostly used to remove old klister and/or kick waxes.

**Whetstone.** For sharpening scrapers (and knives); diamond "stones" last the longest, and if you have a really hard blade such as a cobalt scraper, diamond stones may be the only thing that will do the job. Use a black or blue diamond stone for scrapers; clean with Comet and hot water.

Wire brush or file card. For cleaning files. A small wire brush is best.

# APPENDIX 2

# EQUIPMENT, TOOL, AND WAX SOURCES

The purpose of this appendix is to identify sources for the materials needed for good ski work. All sources listed are ones I have used and can recommend as reliable. Listings are alphabetical, and following each listing I have listed a few of the tools, etc., that the source supplies. All sources do mail-order business, and all publish catalogs.

Akers Ski, Inc.
Box 280
Andover, ME 04216
(207) 392-4582
*Most waxes, annual bargain catalog on closeouts, team discounts, most basic equipment*

Cole Parmer Instrument Company
425 North Oak Park Avenue
Niles, IL 60714
(708) 647-7600
(800) 323-4340
*Scientific equipment; a good source for respirators, hygrometers, thermometers*

Eagle River Nordic
P.O. Box 936
Eagle River, WI 54521
(715) 479-7285
(800) 423-9730
*Most waxes, most basic equipment, well respected for fitting the ski to the skier*

Peter Hale
Box 3764 Bridger Station
Bozeman, MT 59715
(406) 586-9705
fax: (406) 586-9706
*Madshus skis and waxing supplies*

Jenex, Inc.
P.O. Box 1219
Amherst, NH 03031
(603) 672-2600
fax: (603) 672-5751
*Star wax and waxing equipment and supplies, cobalt scrapers, V2 roller skis*

Nordic Equipment, Inc.
Box 997
Park City, UT 84060
(800) 321-1671
*Solda wax, Surgical Tuner Scrapers, ski-tuning video and equipment, training equipment and videos*

New Moon
P.O. Box 132, Highway 63 North
Hayward, WI 54843
(715) 634-8685
(800) 634-8685
*Most waxes, most basic equipment, skis*

Reliable Racing
624 Glen Street, Box A
Glens Falls, NY 12801
(518) 793-5677
(800) 223-4448
*Most waxes, thorough ski-tuning equipment inventory, timing equipment, ski repair equipment*

Tögnar Toolworks (Third Hand)
P.O. Box 212
Mount Shasta, CA 96067
(916) 926-2600
(800) 926-9904
*Large range of ski-tuning tools, most glider waxes, ski repair equipment*

# RECORDING RESULTS, SAMPLE TEST SHEETS

Reproduced here is the glide test sheet I use to record test results as I get them. Please feel free to copy this sample test sheet—and feel equally free to change it in any way to make it meet your own needs. It is better to record more detail, rather than less; there is always something you wish you had noted down.

After testing, I enter the test data and average times in a test log I keep in my laptop. I always add any notes which I feel may be of interest to me later. Wax brands are entered by the first and last letters of their name, thus "Sr" is Star, "Bo" is Briko, etc.

Following the glide test sheet is a sample kick wax test sheet, developed by Jon Quinn-Hurst. Feel free to copy this as well.

## GLIDE TEST RECORD SHEET

Date_____ Time of Day_____
Location_____
Air Temperature_____ Humidity_____
Snow Temperature_____ Dirt Content_____

## Snow Type:
New: Dry, windblown, glazy, damp, saturated
Fine: Packed, moist, saturated
Coarse: Hard, moist, sugar, saturated
Man-made: Hard, packed, moist, sugar, saturated
Mixed: Any of above mixed with man-made

| Ski# | Wax | Speeds | | | | Average |
|---|---|---|---|---|---|---|
| ___ | _____ | ____ | /____ | /____ | /____ | /_____ |
| ___ | _____ | ____ | /____ | /____ | /____ | /_____ |
| ___ | _____ | ____ | /____ | /____ | /____ | /_____ |
| ___ | _____ | ____ | /____ | /____ | /____ | /_____ |
| ___ | _____ | ____ | /____ | /____ | /____ | /_____ |
| ___ | _____ | ____ | /____ | /____ | /____ | /_____ |
| ___ | _____ | ____ | /____ | /____ | /____ | /_____ |
| ___ | _____ | ____ | /____ | /____ | /____ | /_____ |
| ___ | _____ | ____ | /____ | /____ | /____ | /_____ |
| ___ | _____ | ____ | /____ | /____ | /____ | /_____ |
| ___ | _____ | ____ | /____ | /____ | /____ | /_____ |
| ___ | _____ | ____ | /____ | /____ | /____ | /_____ |
| ___ | _____ | ____ | /____ | /____ | /____ | /_____ |
| ___ | _____ | ____ | /____ | /____ | /____ | /_____ |
| ___ | _____ | ____ | /____ | /____ | /____ | /_____ |

Observations:
_____
_____
_____
_____
_____

## SPLIT PAIR KICK WAX TEST FORM

Date_____ Location_____
Condition of the Track_____"Ball Park" Wax_____
Time_____ Temperature_____ Humidity_____
Time_____ Temperature_____ Humidity_____
Time_____ Temperature_____ Humidity_____
Time_____ Temperature_____ Humidity_____
Time_____ Temperature_____ Humidity_____

SPLIT PAIR #
Tester Initials    Ski "A"    Rating*          Ski "B"    Rating
Test 1:            Wax____ K__ G__          Wax____ K__ G___
                   Wax____ K__ G__          Wax____ K__ G__
                   Wax____ K__ G__          Wax____ K__ G__
                   Wax____ K__ G__          Wax____ K__ G__

Test 2:            Wax____ K__ G__          Wax____ K__ G__
                   Wax____ K__ G__          Wax____ K__ G__
                   Wax____ K__ G__          Wax____ K__ G__
                   Wax____ K__ G__          Wax____ K__ G__
Test 3:            Wax____ K__ G__          Wax____ K__ G__
                   Wax____ K__ G__          Wax____ K__ G__
                   Wax____ K__ G__          Wax____ K__ G__
                   Wax____ K__ G__          Wax____ K__ G__

Observations:
_____
_____
_____
_____
_____

* Kick: 1 to 5 (1 = very bad, 5 = perfect "roller-ski kick")
  Glide: 1 to 5 (1 = very bad, 5 = skate-ski glide)

# GLOSSARY

**Binder** is a special wax that has been designed to adhere to the base of the ski, to "glue" kick waxes in place. Most binders won't provide kick, and most will drag if you wear down to them: their sole job is to bind the kick wax to the base. There are both hard wax and klister binders, though the most common klister binders are simply harder klisters, such as blue *skare* (see *Skare*).

**Buffing pads** look like Scotchbrite pads, and are sold under a variety of names. They are used for fine-polishing ski bases. They come in various levels of aggressiveness, finishing off with the least aggressive.

**Camber** is a word used to describe the stiffness, or flex, of a ski. The curve of a ski as it lies on a flat surface is related to its stiffness and feel, and is also referred to as camber.

**Chatter** is a term used to describe small lines created on a ski base by poor scraping, or by scraping with a dull scraper. This is also called "orange skin," which it can resemble.

**Flex** describes the pressure distribution of a ski over its entire surface; you can also refer to "tip flex," "tail flex," etc.

**Fluoroparaffins** are "waxes" with greater or lesser concentrations of fluorocarbons in them, as opposed to "straight" fluorocarbons, which come in the form of powders or solid cakes.

**Form benches** are wooden (sometimes metal) forms that fit the ski and support it along its length. The ski is held in the form by some form of vise or binding clip. Form benches are one of the essential tools.

**"Hair"** is composed of small fibers of base material caused by factory sanding or grinding. Hair on a base slows a ski considerably.

**"Hairies"** are classic skis that have been deliberately sanded in such a way as to produce hair in the kick zone; in conditions of falling snow around 0°C, hairies can provide roller-ski kick when all waxes fail. Hairies work much the same way as mohair.

**Klister** is a sticky wax that comes in "toothpaste" tubes. It is designed for use in snow that has melted and refrozen, or when much water is present, and a wax has to be soft enough for the larger, rounded crystals to dig into it. You can get incredible kick from klisters, but they have bad press owing to their way of oozing all over everything. Put the lid back on the klister tube after using it, and put the tube back in its box.

**Orange skin.** See Chatter.

**Pressure distribution** refers to the way the ski distributes the skier's weight over the surface of the snow. Classic and skating skis call for different distribution patterns, and different snow hardnesses will require different patterns as well. If a ski is too stiff, only the tip and tail will put pressure against the snow, causing the ski to "plow" its way through the snow; or, if the ski is too soft, only the middle section will exert pressure against the snow, and the ski will "wallow" and be unstable. Pressure distribution relates to the skier's weight and to the hardness/softness of the track, as well as to the overall design and construction of the ski.

**P-Tex** is a trade name for the polyethylene plastic most bases are made of.

**Ragging** is using a rolled-up piece of Fiberlene like a paintbrush to spread or mix kick wax: heat the wax with a blowtorch, then "paint" the warm wax with the Fiberlene. Alternate strokes with the Fiberlene with passes of the torch.

**Rills** are various types of small grooves cut or pressed into the base of the ski to relieve suction (see Structure). The most common structure tool is called, simply, a **riller**.

*Skare* is a Scandinavian word for the very hard klisters such as blue, special blue, and green.

**Structure** consists of small grooves, not unlike the grooves on a phonograph record, which are pressed or cut into the base of the ski to relieve suction due to the presence of water. Structure is also sometimes referred to as "texture," but we will use the term "structure" throughout, "structure" having wider currency as well as being for the most part the term most often used internationally.

**Wax pocket** is the area in a classic ski where kick wax is applied. The ski should be stiff enough so that the wax in the kick pocket does not touch the snow while you are gliding, but soft enough so that when you kick, the wax pocket comes into contact with the snow, giving you "kick" or "grip."

# INDEX

# ABOUT THE AUTHOR

Nat Brown taught English and coached high-school cross-country skiing for sixteen years at the Overlake School in Redmond, Washington. He was named Western Regional Coach for the U.S. Biathlon Team in 1979 and waxed the bronze-medal women's relay team at the World Biathlon Championships in 1984. He was wax technician for the U.S. Biathlon Team in 1987–88 and held the same position with the U.S. Cross-Country Team from 1989 to 1993. He was in charge of ski preparation for the Slovene Ski Team at the 1995 and 1999 World Championships. Nat has prepared skis at two Olympics, six World Championships, and seven Junior World Championships and has waxed skis as well for skiers from the Czech Republic, East Germany, Kazakhstan, Slovakia, and Sweden. He edited *Nordic Update* for nine years. He owns and operates Nordic Ultra-Tune Systems, a cross-country-dedicated stone-grinding service, in Edmonds, Washington.

NOTES

THE MOUNTAINEERS, founded in 1906, is a nonprofit outdoor activity and conservation club, whose mission is "to explore, study, preserve, and enjoy the natural beauty of the outdoors. . . . " Based in Seattle, Washington, the club is now the third-largest such organization in the United States, with 15,000 members and five branches throughout Washington State.

The Mountaineers sponsors both classes and year-round outdoor activities in the Pacific Northwest, which include hiking, mountain climbing, ski-touring, snowshoeing, bicycling, camping, kayaking and canoeing, nature study, sailing, and adventure travel. The club's conservation division supports environmental causes through educational activities, sponsoring legislation, and presenting informational programs. All club activities are led by skilled, experienced volunteers, who are dedicated to promoting safe and responsible enjoyment and preservation of the outdoors.

If you would like to participate in these organized outdoor activities or the club's programs, consider a membership in The Mountaineers. For information and an application, write or call The Mountaineers, Club Headquarters, 300 Third Avenue West, Seattle, Washington 98119; (206) 284-6310.

The Mountaineers Books, an active, nonprofit publishing program of the club, produces guidebooks, instructional texts, historical works, natural history guides, and works on environmental conservation. All books produced by The Mountaineers are aimed at fulfilling the club's mission.

Send or call for our catalog of more than 300 outdoor titles:

The Mountaineers Books
1001 SW Klickitat Way, Suite 201
Seattle, WA 98134
800-553-4453
e-mail: mbooks@mountaineers.org
website: www.mountaineersbooks.org

Other titles you may enjoy from The Mountaineers:

**CROSS-COUNTRY SKIING,** Third Ed., *Ned Gillette & John Dostal*
A comprehensive guide covering everything from track to back-country skiing.

**FREE-HEEL SKIING: Telemark and Parallel Techniques for All Conditions,** Second Ed., *Paul Parker*
The fully revised, definitive manual on free-heel skiing, including new techniques, illustrations, and photos.

**BACKCOUNTRY SNOWBOARDING,**
*Christopher Van Tilburg, M.D.*
An introduction to the techniques and concerns of backcountry snowboarding, offering safe ascent and descent techniques for boarding beyond the resort, and illustrated with color photos.

**SNOWSHOEING,** Fourth Ed., *Gene Prater & Dave Felkley*
An essential how-to handbook updated with the latest developments in snowshoeing equipment and techniques, with information on routefinding, camping, and more.

**AVALANCHE SAFETY FOR SKIERS & CLIMBERS,** Second Ed., *Tony Daffern*
A thoroughly illustrated manual stressing the avoidance of avalanche hazard by good routefinding and by recognition of dangerous slopes.

**SECRETS OF WARMTH: For Comfort or Survival,** *Hal Weiss*
If you play outside, work outside, or just commute to work in a cold-weather climate, this book offers tips to keeping warm in all situations.

**CONDITIONING FOR OUTDOOR FITNESS: A Comprehensive Training Guide,** *David Musnick, M.D. & Mark Pierce, A.T.C.*
The most comprehensive guide to conditioning, fitness, and training for all outdoor activities, including programs for hiking, biking, skiing, climbing, paddling, and more.